MW01078567

THE WAY WE EAT

RECIPES FOR HEALTHY LIVING

THE ASHRAM

Cover: Ingredients for Mizuna Niçoise salad, page 76, photo by
Amy Neunsinger.
Endpapers: View of The Ashram garden with the mountains behind,
photo by Price Arana.

© 2018 Assouline Publishing
3 Park Avenue, 27th floor
New York, NY 10016 USA
Tel: 212-989-6769 Fax: 212-647-0005
www.assouline.com

Art director: Charlotte Sivrière
Editorial director: Esther Kremer
Editor: Amy L. Slingerland
Photo editor: Hannah Hayden

ISBN: 9781614286981
Printed in China.
All rights reserved.
No part of this publication may be reproduced or transmitted in any
form or by any means, electronic or otherwise, without prior consent
of the publisher.

Information contained in this Work does not constitute medical advice,
nor is it a substitute for medical advice. Consult a physician regarding
any medical diagnosis or treatment. In no event shall the Publisher or
Authors be liable under any theory of law for any claims of damages.

THE ASHRAM COOKBOOK

Foreword by Cindy Crawford

Introduction by Catharina Hedberg | Food Photography by Amy Neunsinger

Food Styling by Frances Boswell | Produced by Price Arana

THE WAY WE EAT

RECIPES FOR HEALTHY LIVING

Recipes by Suzie Spring Bohannon

ASSOULINE

"THE SECRET TO LIVING WELL
AND LONGER IS: EAT HALF,
WALK DOUBLE, LAUGH TRIPLE,
AND LOVE WITHOUT MEASURE."

TIBETAN PROVERB

TABLE OF CONTENTS

SWEETS & SNACKS

SMOOTHIES & TONICS

CHEEZES, MYLKS, DRESSINGS & SAUCES

NOTE FROM THE CHEF:

Many recipes in this book call for raw unfiltered honey, runny egg yolks, fermented foods, supplements, and so on, which are nutritionally excellent, but may contain bacteria or may be contraindicated for certain conditions or medications. Consult a physician if in any doubt.

FOREWORD
BY CINDY CRAWFORD

I first went to The Ashram when I was 28, heartbroken from a divorce. I was welcomed by Cat's open arms and shown my tiny room. Waking up early for yoga in the dome, I looked around at the eleven strangers sharing this experience with me, nervous about what I had signed up for. The Ashram isn't easy; it definitely takes us all out of our comfort zones. After a small breakfast (and no caffeine!) we pile into a large van and head out for a four-hour hike. The hikes are beautiful, it's the perfect place to think and to make new friends, and you are happy for conversation. In fact, later when I would go with the same group year after year, we would pride ourselves on stretching a five-minute story into a thirty-minute saga, the exact opposite of how we usually tell happenings in regular life.

Returning famished for lunch, we gather around a large table and take a moment to be grateful. This gratitude nourishes us as much as the food, which is healthy, real, mostly raw, and delicious! It's a great opportunity to try out being vegan, and even though the portions look small at first, the meals always end up being just enough to satisfy.

After a blissful hour to nap or sit by the pool, next up is pool volleyball, which is definitely the highlight of the day (along with an incredible massage, which you absolutely need in order to get back on the trails the next morning). This is followed by a strengthening class like Pilates or weights, and then pre-dinner yoga. By dinnertime, everyone is exhausted and so happy to sit down together by the fireplace's flickering light and share a meal together. Once again, we share our gratitude and dig in. The delicious food warms our bellies and souls. Some head off to bed after dinner, but I tend to curl up on the big sectional in front of the fire and get to know my fellow campers. I have met so many incredible people and lifelong friends here. With the publication of *The Way We Eat,* now even more of us can become part of The Ashram community and experience its unique recipes and approach to eating. Thanks, Ashram!

INTRODUCTION

BY CATHARINA HEDBERG

In the early 1970s, as an enthusiastic young Swedish exercise advocate, passionate about inspiring people to move in any way possible, I had been traveling the world for a few years setting up health programs. I had an easy laughter and loved the adventures that I created in my life, and my interest was beginning to turn toward a bigger challenge: America was my next mission.

I had heard of an outrageous Swedish woman in California, Anne Marie Bennstrom, who had already introduced health ideas to Americans with her no-nonsense, ahead-of-the-times ways. A chiropractor, naturopath, and nature girl who lived on fruits, nuts, greens, and grains, she was known for her inspiring lectures and fun TV shows as an outspoken, intuitive force of nature who could make anyone get up and move. I went to look her up and we became fast friends, sharing a passion for health and the vision to bring it forward in a unique form. Through the years she became my most valuable mentor, and where I stand today in my knowledge about nurturing the total being is much because of her.

In 1974 we opened our doors to introduce a whole new concept of health-giving ideas. We called it The Ashram, meaning "a place of peace," and we felt it was a name to live up to. We were the first "boot camp" retreat, and the purpose was to take a handful of guests and educate them in both physical and spiritual ways. This was not an easy task, as Americans in those days did not generally take care of themselves in a healthy way: They did not exercise, and many did not know of the benefits of healthy foods and certainly not about organics.

We made the program simple: Hiking for fresh air and communication with nature, yoga and meditation for soul renewal, and fresh organic food to nurture the body.

We served the food with chopsticks to slow down the eating process. The table was full of pots with growing herbs, and everyone had little scissors to snip their own to flavor their salads—educational and fun! We spent hours in our organic garden teaching guests what they could grow at home and surprisingly even what some vegetables looked like.

Nowadays guests are much more knowledgeable, but they still spend quite some time with our organic gardener learning about the various herbs and edible flowers and how to use them. They return from the garden with handfuls of sweet-smelling roses, lemon balm, thyme, or chocolate mint, and we give them a small vase to put in their rooms to enjoy the aromas.

The Ashram staff is an amazing group of individuals who come with loving hearts. I do not hire anyone because of their résumé, but because they have that special loving, caring energy that cannot be taught. Most of the staff, from massage therapists to housekeepers to instructors, have been with us for decades, some even from the very beginning, and now their grown children work here as well.

When you come to The Ashram, you are immediately welcomed into this family. No need to wear makeup or get dressed up, no pressure to be anything but yourself. The house is comfortable and cozy but not fancy. Our kitchen is wide open, because we want everyone to be able to come and see the food being prepared and to learn as we create the daily meals.

At first, people came to us for weight loss, because the idea of holistic health was quite foreign, and the only way people could understand The Ashram program was through what it did for the body. "How much can I lose?" people asked when they called to reserve a place.

Now, though—especially since 9/11, which started an era of noticeably higher stress—guests have different priorities. They are looking for a place to be quiet, to take time out from families and professional roles, and to stop the clock for a moment. People coming

to The Ashram give themselves a gift of time spent only on themselves, a time to unplug, but also a time to get balanced and set new intentions for the future. Our guests tell me often that it is not really what they lose at The Ashram that is important, but what they gain: a new appreciation for their body's strength and resilience, an inner awakening to solve personal matters in a more balanced way, and very often genuine friendships with other guests and our staff. In fact, more than half our guests each week are returnees.

Our program has always nurtured not only the physical aspect, but also our spiritual and emotional well-being. The day starts with an early morning call for yoga in our geodesic dome by a beautiful bell or one of the staff members' gentle guitar music. Lunch is sometimes served in the garden around a long table with laughter and joy; dessert is a treasure hunt through the strawberry patches or picking whatever fruits are in season. In the evening, we have restorative yoga and meditation or a breathing class to lead us into a place of stillness for the night.

The daily four-to-five-hour hikes in the Santa Monica Mountains are a key ingredient. Every morning we set out early, when the air is still cool and fresh with the smell of pine and eucalyptus, to discover a new path. It is good exercise, but more important, away from the noise of the city, it is a time to quiet the mind, to commune with nature, and to practice walking meditation. People feel lighter as they walk: They may be losing weight, but the lightness also comes from letting go of some issues in their lives that have been weighing them down.

Our vegetarian food works the same way, nurturing all aspects of ourselves. It is nutrient-dense, and most vegetables, depending on the season, are picked in our organic garden just a short walk down the hill, washed and served right away, full of nature's life force. The Ashram has been "farm to table" since long before the term existed. Guests return from hikes or classes to see beautiful plates served amid candles and fresh garden roses. Each dish is a riot of bright reds, greens, yellows, and oranges. We "eat

Herbs From the
Garden !!!

Crush In Your
Fingers And Steep...
Then Enjoy...

the rainbow," as our head chef Suzie says. The food brings joy to the soul as much as it nourishes the body.

We have been adjusting our program slightly over the years. When we started, we were happy if guests could walk up our steep driveway, for people were generally in rather poor shape. We had two short, and mostly flat, hikes a day, and asking people to live simply on plant foods and exercise intensely every day was a new concept. A beauty editor at *Vogue* came to visit our first year and said she could absolutely not write about us because our program of yoga, hiking, and vegetarian food was too outrageous. But a few years later, when we became a popular place for people in the entertainment business to come between movies to get fit, we finally got a six-page layout in *Vogue,* and that opened our doors to plenty of other people who wanted to try this unique program.

Over the decades, our guests' level of fitness has steadily increased, as has their knowledge of food and self-care. We have always stayed ahead of the curve, to make sure we challenge our guests, from triathletes to beginners. Hikes are much longer, but can be individualized. Evening programs vary, but are more informative on deeper levels, such as discussions on the body-soul connection.

Turning to food—the subject of this book—what role does it play? Food is one of the most essential ingredients for holistic health. In our busy lives, it is easy to overlook this basic concept. If we eat when distracted or bored or in a hurry, we do not notice what and how much we consume. Therefore, we encourage mindful eating, and that is the reason for the chopsticks. First-time guests at The Ashram are surprised at what the body can accomplish with much smaller potions, but the fresh organic food is filled with all the nutrients you need, with no empty calories. But of course no one leaves our table hungry; extra helpings are always freely available.

The Ashram has never followed one specific diet. Our food is vegetarian, but not vegan, as we do use products such as eggs and ghee. We serve a lot of raw food to keep

the rainbow as vivid and full of nutrients as possible. We also understand the comfort of a warm dinner with hot soups, roasted root vegetables, and chewy grains. Our food is fresh, vital, and interesting in its form, but I would say the main component of all our dishes is that they are prepared with love and a caring heart. A guest once told me that The Ashram represents kindness and warmth, and when he thinks of the staff and their smiles, he feels that these attributes are reflected in the food and the flavors.

In her recipes, Suzie looks at the big picture—food as life force—and then focuses on the details of the chemistry of the ingredients and how they can serve us. She loves nutrient-rich foods from around the world: West African red palm fruit oil for lycopene and vitamin E, immune-boosting shatavari (also called Indian asparagus), and all kinds of seaweed, which is very rich in vitamins and iodine. She also harnesses the secret powers of more familiar foods like pine nuts and fennel, and boosts the nutritional value of seeds and nuts by sprouting them.

We have included new recipes along with retired classics that guests have praised, such as a hearty Coconut Chipotle soup and a super-energizing (and beautiful) sunflower seed pâté made with raw beets. We also have a seasonal spring-summer program in Mallorca, Spain, and our cooks there have shared some delicious dishes, such as the Tortilla Española. And our third program, the pilgrimage of the Camino de Santiago, also in Spain, has introduced different tastes and ingredients, as seen in the Caldo Gallego soup.

These recipes are not a rigid system. Just as The Ashram weekly program gives guests some tools to live a more balanced life, these recipes are meant to bring flavor, beauty, and health into your life, in whatever way feels right to you. Don't feel that you must rush out and buy all the special ingredients at once. Start with what you have and add laughter and joy. If one recipe seems too tricky, just turn the page and try another.

The Ashram Cookbook is intended to be one of the spokes of the Wheel of Life that all lead to this central hub: the desire for health, peace, and balance in body, mind, and soul.

1
EGGS & BOWLS

CURRIED MOUNTAIN OATS
WITH GINGER FLAX DRESSING

Serves 2-4

2½ cups water

1 cup rolled oats

4 tsp coconut oil

3 tsp Bragg Liquid
   Aminos

1 tsp nutritional yeast

1 tsp curry powder

½ tsp sesame oil

½ tsp freshly ground
   black pepper

½ tsp ground cumin

½ tsp ground turmeric

2 pinches ground
   chipotle

2 pinches ground sweet
   paprika

1 cup nut mylk
   (pages 174, 177)

2 radishes, sliced

½ green apple, sliced

8-inch stalk celery, diced

½ cup Swiss chard,
   minced

2 Tbsp green onion,
   sliced

2 Tbsp flat-leaf parsley,
   minced

2 tsp sesame seeds

1-2 Tbsp Ginger Flax
   Dressing (page 179),
   for serving

- In a pot over medium heat, bring the water to a boil. Add the oats, reduce heat to low, and simmer for 15 minutes, or until the water is gone. Remove from heat.
- To the oats, add the coconut oil, Bragg Liquid Aminos, nutritional yeast, curry powder, sesame oil, black pepper, cumin, turmeric, chipotle powder, and paprika and stir until well blended.
- Using a ½-cup or 1-cup measure, depending on the number of servings, mold the spiced oats into rounded shapes and place in serving bowls.
- Pour equal portions of the nut mylk into each bowl; scatter each serving with radishes, apple, celery, Swiss chard, green onion, parsley, and sesame seeds; and drizzle with Ginger Flax Dressing.

AN EXCELLENT LOW-SODIUM ALTERNATIVE FOR TAMARI AND SOY SAUCE, BRAGG LIQUID AMINOS IS A NON-FERMENTED, GLUTEN-FREE SEASONING MADE FROM NON-GMO SOYBEANS AND PURIFIED WATER THAT CONTAINS SIXTEEN AMINO ACIDS, INCLUDING A SMALL AMOUNT OF GLUTAMIC ACID, A PRECURSOR TO MSG. NATURALLY OCCURRING FREE GLUTAMIC ACID IN SMALL AMOUNTS IS NOT CONSIDERED HARMFUL, AS IT IS THE CHEMICAL COMPOUND IN FOOD THAT CREATES THE SAVORY UMAMI FLAVOR WE ALL KNOW AND LOVE.

SHAKSHUKA

This updated traditional recipe is a snap to prepare, and the addition of fennel and fresh tomatoes offers an improved digestive experience without compromising flavor. Serve hot, preferably with a side salad.

Serves 2

1 Tbsp olive oil

½ cup sweet onion, diced

½ cup fennel, diced

1 clove garlic, minced

3 roma tomatoes, diced

2 Tbsp red bell pepper, minced

½ tsp smoked ground paprika

¼ tsp ground cumin

¼ tsp sea salt

¼ tsp smoked sea salt

¼ tsp freshly ground
black pepper

2 dashes ground clove

2 whole large pasture-raised eggs

1-2 Tbsp Macadamia Ricotta
(page 182)

1 Tbsp fennel fronds, chopped,
for garnish

- Preheat the oven to 375°F. In a small skillet over medium heat, warm the oil. Add onion, fennel, and garlic and sauté for 5-7 minutes, or until lightly browned and fragrant. Remove from heat and set aside.
- In a medium mixing bowl, combine the tomatoes, bell pepper, paprika, cumin, sea salt and smoked sea salt, black pepper, and cloves. Add the sautéed veggies and mix until well combined.
- Divide the contents of the mixing bowl into two 5-inch-diameter ramekins. Gently crack an egg onto each portion and top with crumbled Macadamia Ricotta.
- Transfer the ramekins to the oven and bake for 23 minutes, or until the egg whites are fully cooked but the yolks are still runny. Remove from oven and serve garnished with chopped fennel fronds.

FENNEL IS A HIGHLY MEDICINAL VEGETABLE, DUE TO THE PRESENCE OF SEVERAL ESSENTIAL OILS WITH ANTIMICROBIAL AND ANTIFUNGAL PROPERTIES. FENNEL IS WELL KNOWN FOR SOOTHING THE DIGESTIVE SYSTEM AND STIMULATING GUT MOTILITY, ESPECIALLY WHEN EATEN RAW, BUT IT CAN ALSO REDUCE BODY ODORS, FACILITATE HORMONAL BALANCE (ESPECIALLY IN YOUNG WOMEN), PREVENT CANCER, AND SUPPORT THE IMMUNE SYSTEM WITH ITS HIGH VITAMIN C CONTENT AS WELL. FENNEL ALSO STIMULATES THE FLOW OF DIGESTIVE JUICES, IMPROVING THE DIGESTION OF ANYTHING EATEN WITH IT.

BREAKFAST BOWL OF LOVE

Give this bowl an extra boost with any or all of the following: 1 Tbsp cacao nibs, 1 Tbsp goji berries, 2 tsp ground flax or chia seeds, 1 tsp local bee pollen, or ½ tsp E3Live AFA Crystal Flakes.

Serves 1

½ green apple, shredded

¼ cup fennel, shredded

¼ cup untoasted coconut shreds or flakes

5 raw macadamia nuts, pecans, or walnuts, chopped or crushed

1 Tbsp dried cranberries, sweetened with apple juice

½ Tbsp raw pumpkin seeds

3 dashes ground cinnamon

⅔ cup assorted berries, fresh *or* frozen and thawed

¼ tsp lemon zest

¾ cup nut or seed mylk (pages 166, 174, 177)

• Craft your breakfast one ingredient at a time until you have a small mountain of love rising from your bowl.

• Top with berries and lemon zest and finish with the nut or seed mylk of your choice.

PUMPKIN SEEDS ARE A NUTRITIONAL POWERHOUSE, PROTEIN-PACKED AND FULL OF NUTRIENTS FROM COPPER TO MAGNESIUM TO ZINC. THESE LITTLE GREEN WONDERS ARE ALSO RICH IN ANTIOXIDANT PHYTOSTEROLS, WHICH NATURALLY BALANCE CHOLESTEROL LEVELS. BENEFICIAL TO THE HEART, LIVER, ENDOCRINE, AND IMMUNE SYSTEMS, PUMPKIN SEEDS CAN ALSO HELP BOTH MEN AND WOMEN FIND HORMONAL BALANCE—THE HIGH ZINC CONTENT PREVENTS EXCESS ESTROGEN FROM CONVERTING INTO HARMFUL FORMS OF TESTOSTERONE.

EGGIE TACOS
WITH CILANTRO DE GALLO SALSA

Makes 4-6 tacos

1 Tbsp coconut oil

⅓ cup shallots, minced

¼ cup red bell pepper, diced

3 leaves lacinato kale,
  finely chopped

Sea salt and freshly ground
  black pepper

2-3 whole large
  pasture-raised eggs

2-3 Tbsp nut mylk
  (pages 174, 177)

2 dashes ground chipotle

2 dashes smoked paprika

1 dash nutmeg, freshly grated

1 dash white pepper

2 Tbsp flat-leaf parsley, minced

4-6 sprouted corn tortillas

1-2 avocados, sliced, for topping

½ head romaine lettuce,
  shredded, for topping

Cilantro de Gallo Salsa
  (page 180), for topping

Ginger Flax Dressing (page 179),
  optional, for topping

• In a skillet with a lid over medium-low heat, warm the oil. Add the shallots and bell pepper and season with salt and black pepper. Sauté, stirring frequently, for 5 minutes, or until the shallots have caramelized. Add the kale and sauté for 3 more minutes.

• In a medium bowl, combine the eggs, nut mylk, chipotle powder, paprika, nutmeg, and white pepper and season with salt and black pepper. Whisk the mixture until frothy.

• Pour the egg mixture over the sautéed veggies, tilting the pan to distribute the eggs across the veggies if needed. Scatter the parsley over the top and cook for 2 minutes, then with a spatula begin flipping, scraping, and scrambling everything together. As soon as the eggs seem mostly done, cover and remove from heat.

• In a dry skillet over low heat or wrapped in foil in a 350°F oven, toast the tortillas.

• Assemble the tacos by placing equal portions of the egg mixture, avocado slices, lettuce, and Cilantro de Gallo Salsa on top of each tortilla. For extra flavor, drizzle a little Ginger Flax Dressing.

THE USE OF CERTIFIED HUMANE PASTURE-RAISED EGGS IS ENCOURAGED, FOR THE SAKE OF THE HEALTH OF BOTH THE CHICKENS AND THE PEOPLE EATING THEIR EGGS. COMPARED TO EGGS FROM CAGED HENS, PASTURE-RAISED EGGS CONTAIN HIGHER AMOUNTS OF VITAMIN A, B-12, K, CHOLINE, FOLATE, RIBOFLAVIN, AND ZINC; ⅓ LESS CHOLESTEROL AND ¼ LESS SATURATED FAT; SEVEN TIMES MORE BETA CAROTENE, THREE TIMES MORE VITAMIN E, TWICE AS MUCH OMEGA-3 FATTY ACIDS, AND THREE TO SIX TIMES THE AMOUNT OF VITAMIN D.

CALABAZA TORTILLA

Serves 2

2 Tbsp Spanish olive oil

4 threads saffron

⅔ cup yam, diced

½ cup butternut squash, diced

½ cup yellow onion, diced

4-5 pinches sea salt

Freshly ground black pepper

3 whole large pasture-raised eggs

1 tsp garlic chives,
    finely chopped

¼ tsp + 1-2 pinches salt

¼ tsp ground smoked paprika

¼ tsp white pepper

2 dashes nutmeg, freshly grated

• In a skillet over medium-low heat, warm 1 Tbsp of oil with the saffron. Add the yam, squash, and onion, and sauté, stirring occasionally, for 10 minutes. Season to taste with 4-5 pinches of salt and a few grinds of black pepper and cook for 10 additional minutes, or until tender and fragrant. Remove from heat and set aside.

• In a medium mixing bowl, combine the eggs, chives, paprika, nutmeg, and remaining salt and black pepper and whisk until frothy. Add skillet contents to the mixing bowl and stir until well combined.

• Return the clean skillet to medium-low heat and warm the remaining 1 Tbsp oil. Add the contents of the bowl to the skillet and cook for 5-10 minutes, until the sides of the mixture set.

• Reduce heat to low, cover, and cook for 5 more minutes, or until the eggs are cooked through. Remove from heat and flip onto a plate. Set aside to cool.

• Slice and serve with Trampo (page 84) and a side salad.

TOPINAMBUR TORTILLA ESPAÑOLA

Serves 2

2 Tbsp olive oil

1 cup Jerusalem artichoke,
    finely chopped

½ cup onion, finely chopped

1 small pinch saffron threads

¼ tsp + 3 pinches salt

¼ tsp + 1 pinch freshly ground
    black pepper

3 whole large pasture-raised eggs

¼ tsp ground sweet paprika

2 dashes nutmeg, freshly grated

• In a skillet with a lid over low heat, warm 1 Tbsp oil. Add the artichoke, onion, and saffron and season with 2 pinches salt and 1 pinch black pepper. Sauté for 15-20 minutes, or until the onion is caramelized and the artichoke is tender. Remove from heat.

• In a medium mixing bowl, combine the eggs, paprika, nutmeg, and remaining salt and black pepper and whisk until frothy. Add skillet contents to the mixing bowl and stir until well combined.

• Return the clean skillet to medium-low heat and warm the remaining 1 Tbsp oil. Add contents of the mixing bowl to the skillet and cook for about 5-10 minutes, or until the sides of the mixture set. Reduce heat to low, cover, and cook for 5 more minutes, or until the eggs are cooked through. Remove from heat, flip onto a plate, and set aside to cool.

• Slice and serve with sliced fresh tomatoes, salad, and Chimichurri (page 179).

UME GREENS
WITH SUNNY-SIDE-UP EGGS

The eggs can also be prepared however you like them best!

Serves 1

1½ Tbsp coconut oil

2 shallots, finely chopped

2 cloves garlic, minced

Sea salt and freshly ground
  black pepper

3 large leaves Swiss chard, with
  stems, coarsely chopped

½ tsp ume plum vinegar

1-2 whole large
  pasture-raised eggs

2-4 dashes nutmeg, freshly
  grated

• In a large skillet over medium-low heat, warm
1 Tbsp coconut oil. Add the shallots and garlic
and season with salt and black pepper.
Sauté for 3-5 minutes, or until golden and fragrant.

• Add the Swiss chard and vinegar and mix.
The chard cooks very quickly, so without hesitation,
push the vegetables to one side of the pan and
crack one or two eggs into the empty half.

• Sprinkle a pinch of salt and 2 dashes of nutmeg
over each egg and cook for 3-5 minutes, until
the whites are cooked but the yolks are still runny.

• Remove from heat, and serve eggs atop the sautéed chard.

CONSUMING RAW OR UNDERCOOKED ANIMAL PRODUCTS ALWAYS CARRIES THE RISK OF FOODBORNE ILLNESS VIA SALMONELLA OR LISTERIA CONTAMINATION, ESPECIALLY IN INDIVIDUALS WITH IMMUNE DEFICIENCIES. THAT BEING SAID, A RUNNY EGG YOLK IS FAR AND AWAY THE HEALTHIEST PART OF THE EGG TO CONSUME. RICH IN VITAMINS A, D, E & K AS WELL AS VALUABLE AND VOLATILE OMEGA-3 FATTY ACIDS AND ANTIOXIDANTS, EGG YOLKS ALSO CONTAIN SATURATED FATS AND CHOLESTEROL THAT WE HAVE NOW COME TO UNDERSTAND ARE NOT THE DEMONS WE ONCE THOUGHT. CHOLESTEROL IS ESSENTIAL TO LIFE. IT PLAYS IMPORTANT ROLES IN CELLULAR FUNCTION, MEMORY, REPAIRING THE ARTERIES, AND REGULATING THE PATHWAYS THAT CELLS USE TO COMMUNICATE; IT IS ALSO THE PRECURSOR TO BOTH VITAMIN D AND BILE ACIDS, THE LATTER OF WHICH THE LIVER CREATES AS PART OF ITS ROLE IN DIGESTION AND DETOXIFICATION. CHOLESTEROL LEVELS RISE IN RESPONSE TO INFLAMMATION, AND GENERALLY NOT FROM EATING SOMETHING THAT CONTAINS SATURATED FAT AND CHOLESTEROL. IT IS FAR MORE IMPORTANT TO TREAT THE UNDERLYING CAUSE OF INFLAMMATION IN THE BODY THAN TO ARTIFICIALLY LOWER THE BODY'S CHOLESTEROL. HIGH CHOLESTEROL LEVELS ARE LIKELY AN INDICATION THE BODY IS TRYING TO REPAIR DAMAGE CAUSED BY INFLAMMATION.

COCONUT CHIA SMOOTHIE BOWL

Serves 1-2

¼ cup chia seeds

1⅓ cups nut mylk
   (pages 174, 177)

3 pinches ground vanilla beans

4 oz frozen young coconut meat

1 small handful spinach
   or Swiss chard

Juice of 1 lime

1-2 tsp raw honey

3 drops tangerine oil

1 kiwi, peeled and sliced

½ cup fresh pineapple, chopped

2-3 Tbsp coconut, shredded

2 Tbsp chopped raw pecans

2 Tbsp cacao nibs

1 Tbsp raw almonds, sliced

1 tsp bee pollen

½ tsp orange zest

• In a glass jar with a tight seal, combine the chia seeds, 1 cup of the nut mylk, and 1 pinch of ground vanilla beans. Stir, seal, and shake well to mix. Refrigerate overnight for optimal results.

• In a powerful blender, combine the coconut meat, spinach, lime juice, honey, vanilla, essential oil, and the remaining ⅓ cup nut mylk. Using the blender's tamping tool to push the ingredients into the blades, blend the mixture until thick and creamy.

• To serve, pour the nut mylk–soaked chia seeds into 1 or 2 bowls, and pour contents of the blender off to one side of the bowl(s). Decorate the bowl with the kiwi, pineapple, shredded coconut, pecans, cacao nibs, almonds, bee pollen, and orange zest.

UNFILTERED RAW HONEY IS PERHAPS THE WORLD'S FIRST SUPERFOOD, CONTAINING TINY AMOUNTS OF POLLEN, BEESWAX, AND PROPOLIS, AN ANTIBACTERIAL AGENT. RICH IN TRACE MINERALS, B VITAMINS, ENZYMES, AND PROBIOTICS, RAW HONEY'S ANTIFUNGAL AND ANTIVIRAL PROPERTIES ALSO MAKE IT AN EXCELLENT TREATMENT FOR WOUNDS, BURNS, ACNE, AND THE COMMON COLD. RAW HONEY CAN ALSO HELP ALLEVIATE LOCAL ALLERGIES AND PROTECT THE LIVER FROM TOXIC COMPOUNDS, IMPROVING THE ABILITY TO REGULATE BLOOD SUGAR. NEVERTHELESS, CONSUMING RAW HONEY ALWAYS COMES WITH THE SMALL CHANCE OF BEING CONTAMINATED WITH CLOSTRIDIUM BOTULINUM SPORES, WHICH ARE READILY FOUND IN NATURE. THEREFORE, RAW UNFILTERED HONEY SHOULD NEVER BE FED TO INFANTS.

QUINOA WITH POT O' BLACK GOLD BEANS, GRILLED ZUCCHINI PLANKS & MOLÉ SAUCE

Not only for breakfast, this dish is a great way to fire up the day from the inside, especially on a cold morning. Almost every component in this meal can be prepared ahead of time.

Toppings for serving
½ avocado, sliced, for serving
¼ cup diced tomato, for serving
Chopped fresh cilantro,
   for garnish
¼ cup Mexican Molé Sauce
   (page 183), for serving

• In individual serving bowls, place ⅓ cup Basic Quinoa, ¼ cup Pot O' Black Gold Beans, and lay 2-3 Grilled Zucchini Planks on top. Garnish with ½ avocado sliced and laid in a fan, ¼ cup diced tomato, and sprinkle with a little chopped fresh cilantro.
• The Mexican Molé Sauce can be served on the side or, for those who are willing to dive into the adventure, poured directly over the top!

BASIC QUINOA

Makes about 3 cups, serves 4-6
2 cups water
1 cup quinoa, rinsed and drained

• In a pot over medium heat, combine the water and quinoa and bring to a boil.
• Reduce the heat to low and cook for about 15 minutes, or until the water is almost completely gone and the bottom of the grains begins to crackle. Remove from the heat and cover until ready to serve.

POT O' BLACK GOLD BEANS

Makes about 3-4 cups, serves 4-10
4-6 cups water
1 cup dried black beans, soaked
   overnight, drained, and rinsed*
2-3 bay leaves
1 tsp dried oregano
¾ tsp sea salt

• In a pot over high heat, add beans and 4 cups water and bring to a boil. Add bay leaves, oregano, and salt. Reduce heat and simmer about 1 hour, or until tender. As beans cook, add more water and salt as needed. Remove from heat. Discard the bay leaves and cover until ready to serve.

* If there isn't time to soak the beans overnight, rinse them and then boil them in 4 cups of water for 2 minutes. Remove from the heat and set aside to soak for 1 hour.

GRILLED ZUCCHINI PLANKS

Makes about 12 planks, serves 4-6

1-2 Tbsp coconut oil

2 zucchini, peeled, trimmed, and cut into ¼-inch-thick planks

1-2 Tbsp tamari

2-3 pinches each smoked sea salt and freshly ground black pepper

• In a large skillet over medium heat, warm the oil. Lay the zucchini planks in the hot skillet, sprinkle with half the tamari, salt, and black pepper, and cook for 3-5 minutes.

• Flip, season again with the remaining tamari, salt, and pepper, and cook for 3 more minutes. Remove from heat and serve hot.

CRANBERRY CACAO NO GRAINOLA

Make a fresh start with this simple homemade breakfast! Reminisce about chocolate cake as you crunch your merry way to the bottom of the bowl.

For serving

1 cup Sprouted Nut Mylk
   (pages 174, 177)
½ cup fresh berries
Freshly grated lemon zest

• In individual serving bowls, combine 1 cup Cranberry Cacao No Grainola, 1 cup Sprouted Nut Mylk, and ½ cup fresh berries, and garnish with a pinch of lemon zest.

CRANBERRY CACAO NO GRAINOLA

Makes about 3 cups

½ cup pecans, coarsely chopped
⅓ cup dried cranberries
¼ cup raw walnuts, ground
¼ cup raw cacao powder
¼ cup raw almonds, sliced
3 Tbsp flax seeds, ground
3 Tbsp raw pumpkin seeds
1 Tbsp chia seeds
1 pinch salt
2 tsp reishi mushroom powder
1 cup Sprouted Nut Mylk pulp
   (left over from the
   mylk-making process;
   pages 174, 177)
2½ Tbsp raw honey
2 Tbsp water
12 drops liquid stevia
½ tsp vanilla extract
½ tsp chocolate extract

• In a medium bowl, combine the pecans; cranberries; walnuts; cacao powder; almonds; flax, pumpkin, and chia seeds; reishi powder; and salt.
• In a separate small bowl, stir together the Sprouted Nut Mylk pulp, honey, water, stevia, vanilla and chocolate extracts.
• Gradually add the wet ingredients to the dry ingredient mixture, stirring until thick, gooey clumps form. Scatter the clumps on 2 small dehydrator trays lined with teflex sheets.
• Dehydrate at 145°F for 2 hours to inhibit the growth of pathogens and rapidly reduce the moisture, then reduce temperature to 115°F and dehydrate for 4 more hours.
• Remove the teflex sheet or parchment paper so more air can circulate, and continue dehydrating at 115°F for 8 more hours, or until dry and crunchy.
• Store in glass jars with a tight seal and include a desiccant packet in each.

2
SOuPS & STEWS

COCONUT CHIPOTLE TOMATO SOUP
WITH AVOCADO MANNA BREAD

For the soup to remain enzymatically active, do not overheat it. This soup should be just gently warmed; its temperature should never exceed 108°F, which is only as warm as a nice, hot bath. To ensure it doesn't get too hot, stir it with a clean hand; but for the experience of something piping hot and delicious on a cold night, this soup is excellent when traditionally heated as well.

Makes about 5 cups, serves 4-6

3½ cups water

⅓ cup sundried tomatoes, chiffonaded

⅓ cup oil-cured black olives, pitted

¼ cup onion, chopped

1 tsp dried chipotle pepper, minced

1 clove garlic, minced

3 tomatoes, diced

2 small carrots, peeled and thinly sliced

1 cup kale, chopped

1 cup zucchini, peeled and chopped

¾ cup celery, chopped

½ cup young coconut meat, washed and chopped

⅓ cup sesame seeds, ground

¼ cup olive oil

¼ cup basil leaves, chopped

¼ cup flat-leaf parsley, chopped

1-inch sprig rosemary, minced

1½ tsp sea salt

½ tsp rubbed sage*

½ tsp smoked paprika

½ tsp ground oregano

½ tsp freshly ground black pepper

Green onions, sliced, for garnish

AVOCADO MANNA BREAD

Manna bread or sprouted sourdough peasant bread, cut into 1-inch-thick slices

Sliced avocado

Sea salt and freshly ground black pepper

Fresh sunflower, clover, radish, or buckwheat sprouts

- In a large pot over low heat, bring the water to just under a simmer. When the water is hot and just a tad steamy, remove from heat, add the sliced sundried tomatoes, olives, onion, chipotle, and garlic. Set aside to soak for 5 minutes.
- Add the remaining ingredients except the green onions. With a potato masher, mash the mixture so the vegetables, coconut, and herbs release their juices.
- Return the pot to low heat and gently warm it to about 108°F. Remove from heat.
- While the soup is heating, toast the bread slices, spread with avocado slices, season with sea salt and black pepper, and top with sprouts.
- Garnish warmed soup with sliced green onions and serve with Avocado Manna Bread.
- Leftover soup can be stored in the refrigerator up to 4 days.

* If using ground dried sage, use about half the quantity specified.

CALDO GALLEGO

An updated, vegetarian version of the classic Spanish soup with collard greens and white beans, this Caldo Gallego offers a portal into the flavors of northern Spain. Warm, comforting, and filling, it's perfect on a cold night. (If Jerusalem artichokes are not available, celery root works great too!) And leftovers can be frozen or gifted in mason jars to friends and neighbors.

Makes about 12 cups, serves 8-12

2 cups dried white beans, soaked overnight, drained, and rinsed

8 cups Kombu Morel Vegetable Stock (page 47)

1 cup sliced Jerusalem artichoke *or* celery root, peeled and cubed

1 cup turnip, cut into thin wedges

8 dried morel mushrooms, soaked, drained, and sliced

3 tsp sea salt

½ tsp freshly ground black pepper

2 Tbsp olive oil, plus more for drizzling

1 sweet onion, finely chopped

2 cloves garlic, minced

2 cups (about 4 leaves) collard greens, coarsely chopped

½ cup dandelion greens, chopped

Sprouted sourdough peasant bread, for serving

• In a large skillet over medium heat, warm the oil. Add the onion and garlic and sauté for 5-10 minutes, or until they are translucent and slightly caramelized. Remove from heat.

• Transfer skillet contents to a large slow cooker, add soaked beans, and cover with the Kombu Morel Vegetable Stock. Add the Jerusalem artichoke (*or* celeriac), turnip wedges, morels, and 1 tsp sea salt and cook on high for 4-4½ hours, or until the beans are soft but not falling apart.

• About 20 minutes before serving, add the collard and dandelion greens, season with the remaining 2 tsp sea salt and ½ tsp black pepper, or to taste. Reduce the slow cooker setting to warm.

• Serve hot drizzled with olive oil and sprouted sourdough peasant bread.

• Leftover soup can be stored in the refrigerator for up to 1 week or in the freezer for up to 3 months.

44

KOMBU DASHI

This is a beautiful vegetarian dashi for use in miso soup and nimono dishes.

Makes 1 quart
4½ cups water
½ oz dried kombu*

* IF THERE IS WHITE POWDER ON THE KOMBU, RESIST THE TEMPTATION TO RINSE IT OFF, BECAUSE IT ACTUALLY CONTAINS CRUCIAL UMAMI FLAVORING COMPONENTS!

• In a pot over medium heat, combine the water and kombu and bring to a boil. Boil for 10 minutes, then reduce heat to a simmer for 30 more minutes. Remove from heat.
• Remove the kombu from the pot. (Rather than discarding, it can be used to make a second batch of dashi if desired). If necessary, strain the dashi through a mesh strainer. If the dashi has reduced to less than 4 cups, feel free to add more water.
• Use immediately in a recipe or store in a sealed glass jar in the refrigerator for up to 5 days.

KOMBU MOREL VEGETABLE STOCK

Makes 2 quarts
10 cups water
1 leek, halved
1 white onion, halved
2 carrots, halved
3 stalks celery, halved
1 parsnip, halved
2 shallots, halved
8 dried morel mushrooms
5-6 sprigs thyme
1 handful flat-leaf parsley, chopped
1 strip dried kombu
2 cloves garlic, mashed
1 tsp black peppercorns
1 bay leaf

• In a medium stockpot, combine all ingredients and bring to a boil. Reduce heat to simmer for 1 hour. Remove from heat.
• Using a slotted spoon and strainer, remove all vegetables and seasonings (the morels can be saved for another use, if desired).
• Use immediately in a recipe or store in tightly sealed glass jar(s) in the refrigerator for up to 5 days. Can also be frozen for up to 3 months.

FROM AN EPICUREAN PERSPECTIVE, MOREL MUSHROOMS ARE ONE OF THE MOST PRIZED FUNGI ON THE PLANET, BUT THEIR NUTRITIONAL BENEFITS ARE OFTEN OVERSHADOWED BY THEIR CULINARY CACHET. MORELS ARE RICH IN SELENIUM, FIBER, VITAMIN D, BETA-GLUCANS, AND THE "MASTER ANTIOXIDANTS" GLUTATHIONE AND ERGOTHIONEINE, WHICH NEUTRALIZE FREE-RADICAL DAMAGE, ELIMINATE ENVIRONMENTAL TOXINS, AND PROTECT BRAIN CELLS. MORELS ALSO CONTAIN A POLYSACCHARIDE CALLED GALACTOMANNAN, WHICH HAS THE IMMUNE-STIMULATING CAPACITY TO ENHANCE MACROPHAGE ACTIVITY.

CREAM OF MAITAKE MUSHROOM SOUP

This is a gently warmed, enzymatically active soup. If not served immediately, it can be lightly reheated on the stove before serving, but try not to heat it above 108°F. Commonly known as "hen of the woods," the maitake mushroom has potent antiviral, anticarcinogenic, and immune-boosting properties. As part of a liquid and blended-foods cleanse, this soup is excellent for dinner. The fats in the almond butter combined with the mushrooms make a perfect evening meal, to feel light but nourished for a good night's sleep.

Makes 2 cups, serves 2-4

½ oz fresh maitake mushrooms, minced

1 tsp ume plum vinegar

¼ oz dried porcini mushrooms

⅙ oz dried maitake mushrooms

⅛ cup sweet onion, diced

1⅔ cups hot water, about 108°F

2 Tbsp almond butter

⅛ tsp salt

⅛ tsp freshly ground black pepper

2 pinches thyme leaves, minced

2 tsp flat-leaf parsley, minced, for garnish

1 sprig rosemary, for garnish

Black truffle oil, for garnish

• In a small bowl, combine the fresh maitake mushrooms and vinegar and set aside to marinate for 30 minutes.

• In a separate bowl, combine 1 cup hot water, dried mushrooms, and onion and set aside to steep for 15 minutes.

• In a high-power blender, combine the remaining ⅔ cup hot water, almond butter, salt, ⅛ tsp black pepper, and thyme. Add the contents of both bowls to the blender and puree, first on low then gradually raising the speed to high, until the mixture is smooth and creamy.

• Serve warm, garnished with parsley, rosemary, and a few drops of black truffle oil, and season with black pepper to taste.

EDIBLE FUNGI HAVE A LONG HISTORY OF HELPING HUMANS WARD OFF CANCER, AGING, AND DISEASE, WHILE THEIR SAVORY UMAMI FLAVOR IS ONE OF THE THINGS FOR WHICH THEY ARE MOST PRIZED! MUSHROOMS ARE RICH IN CALCIUM, COPPER, IRON, NIACIN, PHOSPHORUS, POTASSIUM, SELENIUM, AND ZINC; CHOLINE; AND VITAMINS B, C, AND NOTABLY D, WHICH THEY PRODUCE IN RESPONSE TO SUNLIGHT. SELENIUM PERFORMS A NUMBER OF BENEFICIAL FUNCTIONS: IT AIDS IN THE MANUFACTURE OF GLUTATHIONE (GSH), IS ANTI-INFLAMMATORY, AND STIMULATES THE PRODUCTION OF KILLER T-CELLS. MUSHROOMS CONTAIN BENEFICIAL FIBERS LIKE BETA-GLUCANS, WHICH STIMULATE THE IMMUNE SYSTEM AND HELP SLOW THE GROWTH OF TUMORS. AS A DIETARY FIBER, BETA-GLUCANS INCREASE THE FEELING OF SATIETY, CURBING THE DESIRE TO OVEREAT. BUT BECAUSE THE CELL WALLS OF MUSHROOMS ARE INDIGESTIBLE TO HUMANS, HEAT OR BLEND THEM TO ACCESS THE VITAL NUTRIENTS.

LEMON SPICED CHICKPEA & FENNEL STEW

Makes about 8 cups, serves 6-8

7 cups water

1 small sweet onion, cut in sixths, attached at the bottom

1 parsnip, trimmed and peeled

1 carrot, trimmed, peeled, and cut crosswise in fourths

2 stalks celery, cut crosswise in fourths

1 cup dried chickpeas, soaked overnight, drained, rinsed

1 Tbsp coconut oil

½ cup sweet onion, diced

1 shallot, finely chopped

1 large or 2 small fennel bulbs, trimmed, halved, and sliced thin with core attached

2 Tbsp preserved lemon

1 tsp ground cumin

½ tsp ground sweet paprika

4 dashes ground cayenne

2 Tbsp lemon juice

½ cup flat-leaf parsley, chopped

1-2 tsp salt

1 tsp lemon zest, plus extra for garnish

½ tsp freshly ground black pepper

¼ cup olive oil, for drizzling

2 avocados, cubed, for serving

• In a slow cooker, combine 7 cups water, whole sweet onion, parsnip, carrot, celery, chickpeas, and 1 tsp salt, and set to cook on high for 6 hours.

• About 3 hours into the cook time, in a large skillet over medium-low heat, warm the coconut oil and add the diced onion, shallot, preserved lemon, cumin, paprika, cayenne, and two pinches of salt, and sauté for 5-10 minutes. Add the fennel to the skillet and sauté 10 more minutes, or until golden brown. To the skillet, add 1 cup of liquid from the slow cooker, and the lemon juice. Cover and simmer for 15 more minutes, and remove from heat.

• Add skillet contents to the slow cooker, and cook for 2½ more hours, or until the cooking time is up.

• About 15 minutes before serving, add lemon zest and chopped parsley, and salt and pepper to taste.

• Drizzle the olive oil over the stew, and garnish each serving bowl with ¼ fresh cubed avocado, a pinch of lemon zest, and a little freshly ground black pepper.

• Can be served with toasted gluten-free rice bread and Shatavari Ginger Honey Butter (page 187).

• Leftover stew can be stored in the refrigerator up to 1 week, in the freezer for up to 3 months, or gifted in a mason jar to friends.

CHICKPEAS ARE A MEDICINAL TREASURE TROVE, WITH NUMEROUS ANTIOXIDANTS, MINERALS, AND VITAMINS. FERMENTABLE FIBERS IN LEGUMES HELP KEEP METABOLISM IN CHECK AND ENHANCE THE DIGESTIVE AND IMMUNE SYSTEMS. THESE FIBERS STIMULATE PROBIOTICS, STABILIZE BLOOD SUGAR, BALANCE TRIGLYCERIDE AND CHOLESTEROL LEVELS BY INHIBITING INFLAMMATION, PROTECT AGAINST THE FORMATION OF CANCEROUS POLYPS IN THE GUT, AND THEY CAN ALSO HELP TREAT AND PREVENT IBS, CROHN'S DISEASE, AND ULCERATIVE COLITIS.

SUMMER GAZPACHO

Makes 1½ quarts

3 cups tomatoes, peeled and chopped

2 cups organic yellow corn kernels, frozen

1 cup water

½ cup celery leaves, chopped

½ cup basil leaves

3 Tbsp lemon juice

2 Tbsp flat-leaf parsley, minced

2 Tbsp Bragg Liquid Aminos

2 Tbsp olive oil

1 clove garlic

¼ tsp sea salt

¼ tsp white pepper

1½ avocados, diced, for garnish

¼ cup minced chives, for garnish

Manna bread, cut into 1-inch slices and toasted, for serving

3 stalks celery, cut into matchsticks, for serving

½ jicama, peeled and cut into matchsticks, for serving

1 cucumber, peeled and sliced into wedges, for serving

• In a blender or a food processor, combine the tomatoes, corn, water, celery, basil leaves, lemon juice, parsley, Bragg Liquid Aminos, oil, garlic, salt, and white pepper, and pulse into a chunky slush.

• Serve cold or gently warmed on the stove, garnished with the avocado and chives and alongside the manna bread, celery, jicama, and cucumber to make a full, yet simple and satisfying meal.

• Leftover soup can be stored in the refrigerator up to 4 days—or have a mason-jar picnic in the park with a friend.

NUMEROUS STUDIES CONFIRM THAT DAILY CONSUMPTION OF W3 TO 2 CUPS OF PLUMP, JUICY, FRESH TOMATO REDUCES BOTH LDL CHOLESTEROL AND TRIGLYCERIDES, AS WELL IMPROVES BLOOD VESSEL WALL RESPONSIVENESS. TOMATOES ARE RICH IN VITAMINS A, C, & E, CHROMIUM, MANGANESE, AND ZINC, NOT TO MENTION SPECIAL SOLANACEOUS ALKALOIDS AND PHYTONUTRIENT CAROTENOIDS, WHICH OFFER PROTECTION TO THOSE WHO LIKE TO FROLIC IN THE SUN. BETA-CAROTENE, LUTEIN, LYCOPENE, NEUROSPORINE, PHOTOFLUENE, AND ZEAXANTHIN ARE ALL PIGMENT-BASED ANTIOXIDANTS IN TOMATOES THAT GET DEPOSITED RIGHT INTO YOUR SKIN CELLS! THESE CAROTENOIDS ARE VERY STABLE, LITERALLY BLEEDING THEMSELVES DRY OF THEIR PIGMENT AS THEY GO TO WORK QUENCHING THE FIRES OF CELLULAR DAMAGE STARTED BY FREE RADICALS. TOMATO CONSUMPTION LESSENS SKIN REDNESS AFTER UV EXPOSURE, REDUCING THE RISK OF SUNBURN AND PROTECTING AGAINST SKIN CANCER. IMPORTANT: LYCOPENE IS FAT-SOLUBLE, SO TO FULLY ACCESS THE ANTIOXIDANT BENEFITS, TOMATOES MUST BE EATEN WITH A FAT SUCH AS OLIVE OIL OR AVOCADO.

MISO MOREL STEW

Serves 2-4

⅔ cup portobello mushrooms, thinly sliced

⅓ cup oyster mushrooms, finely chopped

⅓ cup shiitake mushrooms, finely chopped

6 dried morel mushrooms, soaked, drained, and sliced

2 Tbsp olive oil

1 Tbsp tamari

2 tsp aged balsamic vinegar

2½ cups water, room temperature

⅔ cup carrot, thinly sliced

⅔ cup summer squash, thinly sliced

½ cup Jerusalem artichoke, thinly sliced

⅓ cup celery, thinly sliced

¼ cup shallot, finely chopped

4 cloves garlic, minced

1 tsp sage leaves, minced

1 tsp rosemary leaves, minced

5 Tbsp unpasteurized white miso

½ cup warm water

1 cup Swiss chard, minced

¼ cup flat-leaf parsley, minced

2 tsp smoked sea salt

½ tsp freshly ground black pepper

½ tsp black truffle oil

Avocado Manna Bread (page 43), for serving

• In a large bowl, combine mushrooms, olive oil, tamari, and balsamic vinegar. Set aside to marinate for 30 minutes.

• In a large pot over medium heat, bring the 2½ cups water to a boil. Remove from heat. Add the carrot, summer squash, Jerusalem artichoke, celery, shallot, garlic, sage, and rosemary and set aside to steep for 10 minutes.

• In a small bowl, whisk together the miso and ½ cup warm water until well combined.

• Add the mushrooms and marinating liquid to the large pot. Add the miso-water mixture, Swiss chard, parsley, salt, black pepper, and truffle oil. Vigorously mash the mixture, releasing the vegetable juices into the broth.

• If the soup has cooled, carefully re-warm it over low heat to no more than 108°F, to preserve the beneficial enzymes. Remove from heat and serve with Avocado Manna Bread for a hearty meal.

• Leftover stew can be stored in a sealed container in the refrigerator for up to 4 days.

SOY IN ITS UNFERMENTED STATE IS NOT SO HEALTHFUL, BUT THE FERMENTED GOODNESS OF MISO IS A WHOLE 'NOTHER STORY. THE LONG, SLOW FERMENTATION PROCESS BY THE KOJI CULTURE BREAKS DOWN THE ANTINUTRIENTS NATURALLY PRESENT IN SOY, BLOOMS THE NUTRIENT CONTENT (HELLO, VITAMIN E!), UNLOCKS SOY PROTEIN'S AMINO ACIDS, AND BASICALLY TRANSFORMS SOYBEANS INTO A PROBIOTIC SUPERFOOD. IN JAPAN, MISO SOUP IS EATEN FOR BREAKFAST, LUNCH, AND DINNER, AND USED AS A SPREAD, IN DRESSINGS, AND AS AN ALL-AROUND "ÜBER-CONDIMENT." CAN YOU EAT TOO MUCH MISO? NOT LIKELY. A REPORT PUBLISHED IN THE JOURNAL OF THE NATIONAL CANCER INSTITUTE IN 2003 DEMONSTRATED THAT EATING A BOWL OF MISO SOUP THREE (OR MORE) TIMES A DAY CUTS THE RISK OF BREAST CANCER IN HALF.

SPARTAN SOUP

The discipline of the ancient Greek city-state of Sparta has been revered for thousands of years. The word *spartan* has become synonymous with fearlessness, endurance, and austerity. The simplicity of this warrior soup embodies all of that. Only the truly brave eat it without salt—the rest of us enjoy it with some smoked alderwood salt, like a hot ration gifted from the campfire after a long day on the trail.

Serves 4-6

6 cups water

1 cup sweet potato, peeled and cubed

1 cup broccoli florets and stems, cubed

½ cup zucchini squash, peeled and cubed

¼ cup carrot, peeled and sliced

2½ cups green cabbage, chopped

4 oz green beans, chopped

1½ oz kale, stemmed and chopped

2 tsp chili powder

½ tsp smoked paprika

2-3 Tbsp olive oil

2 avocados, sliced, for garnish

⅓ cup flat-leaf parsley, minced, for garnish

¼ cup dehydrated sprouted sunflower seeds, for garnish

Alderwood-smoked (if available) sea salt

- In a large pot, combine all vegetables and cover with 6 cups water. Bring to a boil, then reduce heat to simmer for about 20 minutes, or until sweet potato is tender.
- Transfer ⅓ of the mixture to a blender and puree until smooth.
- Return contents of blender to the pot, add the chili powder and paprika, and simmer on low heat for 15-20 more minutes, or until the consistency of the soup is hearty and thick.
- Garnish with olive oil, avocado slices, parsley, sunflower seeds, and alderwood-smoked sea salt to taste. May be served with organic brown rice cakes topped with tomato slices on the side.

IN CHINESE MEDICINE, COOKED STARCHY, EARTHY VEGETABLES SUCH AS YAMS AND SQUASH NOURISH THE SPLEEN-PANCREAS NETWORK, STIMULATING THOSE ORGANS TO PARTICIPATE IN ENZYMATIC DIGESTION. STIMULATING THE SPLEEN HELPS TO RID "DAMPNESS" FROM THE BODY, AS THE SPLEEN IS OFTEN VIEWED AS THE ENERGETIC TOUCHSTONE OF QI, THE LIFE-FORCE ENERGY. ANTIBIOTICS, SEDENTARY LIFE, CONSUMING COLD FOODS AND BEVERAGES, AND GENERAL STRESS CAN LEAD TO A DEFICIENT SPLEEN, AND THE RESULTING DAMPNESS THAT FOLLOWS FROM VIRAL, BACTERIAL, AND FUNGAL IMBALANCES CAN LEAVE ONE FEELING PHYSICALLY AND MENTALLY FATIGUED AND ANXIOUS, WITH A COMPROMISED DIGESTIVE SYSTEM.

SIMPLICITY BROTH

Makes about 1 quart

5 cups water

2 carrots, halved

½ onion, skin on, quartered

1 stalk celery, halved

3 sundried tomato halves

2 bay leaves

1 Tbsp dried porcini, chopped

1 tsp salt (optional)

- In a large pot over medium heat, combine all ingredients. Boil for 20-30 minutes, or until fragrant and richly colored.
- Remove from heat, strain broth into a separate container, and discard the solids.
- Use immediately in a recipe, or store in a sealed container in the refrigerator for up to 1 week. Can also be frozen for up to 3 months.

OF ALL MUSHROOMS, PORCINIS CONTAIN THE MOST ERGOTHIONEINE AND GLUTATHIONE, "MASTER ANTIOXIDANTS" THAT THWART OXIDATIVE STRESS, CLEANSE HEAVY METALS AND TOXINS FROM THE BLOOD, AND MAINTAIN INTRACELLULAR HEALTH. ERGOTHIONEINE IS BELIEVED TO HELP PREVENT NEURODEGENERATIVE DISEASES LIKE PARKINSON'S AND ALZHEIMER'S, WHILE GLUTATHIONE IS NOW WIDELY BELIEVED TO BE A GENERAL PREDICTOR OF LONGEVITY.

LENTIL SOUP

Makes 4½ cups, serves 4-6

2 tsp olive oil

½ cup leek, white and green parts, sliced thin

1 small clove garlic, minced

½ cup dried green lentils

1 tsp sea salt

½ tsp freshly ground black pepper

4 cups water

½ cup carrots, chopped

½ cup onion, finely chopped

2 oz green beans, ends trimmed and cut in fourths

⅓ cup zucchini, diced

⅓ cup celery, chopped

⅓ cup Swiss chard, finely chopped

- In a large pot over low heat, warm the oil. Add the leek and sauté for 8-10 minutes. Raise heat to medium, add the garlic, and cook for 2 minutes, or until golden.
- Add the lentils, a pinch of salt and pepper, and cook, stirring constantly, for 2 minutes, add 2 cups water, bring to a boil, and simmer for 20 more minutes on medium-low.
- Add carrots, onion, green beans, zucchini, celery, and 2 cups water, return to a boil, then simmer for 15 more minutes on medium-low.
- Before serving, add the Swiss chard, and adjust seasoning to taste.
- Leftover soup can be stored in the refrigerator up to 1 week.

GREENS & SALADS

ARAME & BEETS

Makes 3 cups, serves 2-4

1 cup dried arame seaweed
Water, as needed
2 small Chioggia beets, peeled and julienned with a mandoline
½ cup beet greens, washed and chopped
2 green onions, sliced
2-3 Tbsp lemon juice

2 Tbsp flaxseed oil
2 Tbsp tamari
1 Tbsp fresh ginger, peeled and minced
1 Tbsp shiso leaves, minced
2 tsp hot sesame oil
1½ tsp ume plum vinegar
Sliced avocado and green salad, for serving

• In a small bowl, cover the arame with water and soak for 15 minutes, or until pliable.
• Drain the arame. In a medium serving bowl, combine all ingredients except the avocado and green salad and toss until well combined.
• Serve with avocado and green salad, or store in a sealed container in the refrigerator for up to 3 days.

LOADED WITH IRON, RED BEETS ARE A TASTY WAY TO REPLENISH IRON IN THE BLOODSTREAM. AND THE BIOAVAILABLE IODINE FOUND IN ARAME CAN HELP REGULATE THYROID FUNCTION. THIS BROWN SEAWEED HAS POWERFUL CHELATING PROPERTIES DUE TO ITS SODIUM ALGINATE CONTENT, WHICH DRAWS AND BINDS WITH RADIOACTIVE PARTICLES AND HEAVY METALS SO THEY CAN PASS HARMLESSLY FROM THE BODY.

KINPIRA
BURDOCK & CARROT SALAD

Makes 3 cups, serves 2-4

2 8-inch burdock (*gobo*) roots, peeled and finely julienned
2 8-inch carrots, peeled and finely julienned
4 Tbsp black sesame seeds, toasted

2 Tbsp lemon juice
4 tsp rice vinegar
3 tsp hot sesame oil
3 tsp ume plum vinegar
2 tsp tamari

• In a medium mixing bowl, combine all ingredients, cover with plastic wrap, and let marinate overnight to soften the burdock and carrot.
• Serve or store in a sealed container in the refrigerator for up to 1 week.

TRADITIONALLY, THIS JAPANESE DISH IS BRAISED, BUT WHEN SERVED RAW, IT IS PACKED WITH HEALTH BENEFITS. EVEN IN SMALL AMOUNTS, IT PROVIDES INTERESTING FLAVOR AND TEXTURE TO MAIN COURSES.

OAXACA RANCH SALAD

Serves 2-4

2 small heads romaine or butter lettuce

10 cherry tomatoes, halved

1 Persian cucumber, sliced

2 radishes, thinly sliced

2 stalks celery, sliced

2 ears corn kernels

1 cup jicama, julienned

½ cup white onion, diced

½ avocado, sliced

6 Tbsp fresh cilantro, chopped, for garnish

6 Tbsp pumpkin seeds, toasted, for garnish

4 Tbsp Macadamia Ricotta (page 182), for garnish

2 dashes ground chipotle, for garnish

Oaxaca Ranch Dressing, for serving

- In a large salad bowl, arrange lettuce leaves then add tomatoes, cucumber, radishes, celery, corn, jicama, onion, and avocado.
- Garnish with cilantro, pumpkin seeds, Macadamia Ricotta, and chipotle powder, and drizzle with Oaxaca Ranch Dressing.

OAXACA RANCH DRESSING

Makes about 2 cups

¼ cup raw cashews, soaked 3-5 hours, rinsed, and drained

¼ cup raw pine nuts, soaked 2-3 hours, rinsed, and drained

¼ oz shallots, chopped

3 Tbsp lemon juice

2 Tbsp olive oil

2 Tbsp flaxseed oil

1½ Tbsp raw tahini

1 Tbsp white balsamic vinegar

1 small clove garlic

2 tsp tamarind, destemmed, deseeded (directions, page 90) *or* 2 tsp tamarind paste

2 tsp maple syrup

1 tsp salt

1 tsp nutritional yeast

¼ tsp smoked paprika

⅛ tsp chipotle powder

2 dashes ground cayenne

2 pinches ground clove

¾ cup water

1 tsp dried parsley

1 tsp dried dill weed

1 tsp fresh chives, minced

- In a high-power blender, combine all ingredients except the water, parsley, dill, and chives. Add ¼ cup water and puree, first on low then gradually raising the speed to high, until mixture is very smooth and creamy. Add the remaining ½ cup of water to thin the mixture and blend again.
- Transfer to a glass jar and stir in the parsley, dill, and chives. Use immediately or seal and store in the refrigerator for up to 1 week.

DESIGNED TO EMULATE FAMILIAR ELEMENTS OF RANCH DRESSING, THIS RECIPE HAS A LOT OF INGREDIENTS BECAUSE IT IS MADE FROM SCRATCH WITH LOVE. IF PRESSED FOR TIME, TAMARIND PASTE MAY BE SUBSTITUTED, BUT THE PROCESS OF WORKING WITH FRESH TAMARIND IS A FUN SLOW-FOOD EXPERIENCE.

CELERY WALDORF SALAD
WITH ZESTY HONEY LEMON CASHEW DRESSING

Can be served with a green salad or alone garnished with watercress.

Serves 2-4

2-4 cups water, as needed

2 Tbsp freshly squeezed lemon juice

2 green apples, cored and sliced into thin ringlets

1 cup burdock (*gobo*) root, peeled and diced

6 celery stalks, thinly sliced crosswise

½ cup inner celery leaves, chopped

1 cup raw walnuts, chopped

½ cup dried cranberries, sweetened with apple juice

1 cup flat-leaf parsley, minced

2 Tbsp lemon zest

Freshly ground black pepper

Zesty Honey Lemon Cashew Dressing, for drizzling

Green salad, for serving (optional)

Watercress leaves, for garnish (optional)

• Before prepping apple and burdock root, combine water and lemon juice in a medium mixing bowl.

• Immediately after cutting the apple and burdock, immerse in the lemon water to prevent oxidation. Drain just before adding to salad.

• In a large serving bowl, combine celery stalks and leaves, walnuts, cranberries, and parsley, add the drained apple and burdock, and season with lemon zest and black pepper. Drizzle with Zesty Honey Lemon Cashew Dressing and toss gently to coat.

ZESTY HONEY LEMON CASHEW DRESSING

Makes ¾ cup

½ cup raw cashews, soaked 2-4 hours, drained, and rinsed

⅓ cup water

2 Tbsp lemon juice

1½ Tbsp olive or flaxseed oil

½ Tbsp white wine vinegar

1 Tbsp raw honey

2 tsp apple cider vinegar

½ tsp freshly ground black pepper

½ tsp sea salt

1 dash white pepper

• In a high-power blender, combine all ingredients and puree, first on low then gradually raising the speed to high, until smooth and creamy.

• Use immediately or transfer to a glass jar with a tight seal, and store in the refrigerator for up to 5 days.

FEISTY BREADCRUMB SALAD
& WALNUT MYLK BLACK PEPPER DRESSING

EZEKIEL 4:9 BREAD IS A FLOURLESS BREAD MADE FROM SPROUTED WHOLE GRAIN MILLET, WHEAT, BARLEY, LENTILS, SOYBEANS, AND SPELT, AS WELL AS OTHER SEEDS AND GRAINS. SPROUTING GRAIN PRIOR TO GRINDING IT INTO MEAL FOR BAKING BREAD INCREASES THE DIGESTIBILITY AND BIOAVAILABILITY OF ANTIOXIDANTS, VITAMINS, AND MINERALS. FLOURLESS BREAD IS ALSO INHERENTLY LOWER IN CARBOHYDRATES, MAKING IT DIABETIC-FRIENDLY.

66

Serves 2-4

1 shallot, sliced very thinly

2 tsp ume plum vinegar

2 cups water

Juice of ½ lemon

12-inch piece burdock (*gobo*) root,
    peeled and sliced into ribbons

1 head romaine lettuce

1 cup flat-leaf parsley, minced

2 cups Feisty Breadcrumbs

1 stalk celery, cut crosswise

8 oz fresh blackberries

2-4 pinches red chili flakes

Walnut Mylk Black Pepper Dressing,
    for drizzling

- In a small bowl, combine the shallot and vinegar and set aside to marinate for about 20 minutes until softened while prepping everything else.
- Before prepping burdock root, combine water and lemon juice in a medium mixing bowl.
- Peel and discard the dark outer skin of the burdock root, exposing the white flesh. Peel the entire root into long ribbons and transfer immediately to the lemon water to prevent oxidation. Drain just before adding to salad.
- In a large serving bowl, assemble the salad by first adding the lettuce and then the parsley, Feisty Breadcrumbs, drainedburdock root, celery, blackberries, chili flakes, and shallot with vinegar marinade. Drizzle with Walnut Mylk Black Pepper Dressing and serve.

FEISTY BREADCRUMBS

Makes 2 cups

6 pieces Ezekiel 4:9 bread, torn into
    bite-size chunks

½ cup olive oil

3 tsp harissa powder

Sea salt and freshly ground
    black pepper

- Preheat the oven to 400°F. In a mixing bowl, toss all ingredients until well coated, squeezing the bread chunks to soak up the oil.
- On a baking sheet lined with parchment paper, spread bread chunks in a single layer and bake for 15 minutes, or until browned but still slightly chewy. Remove from oven and set aside to cool.
- Use immediately or transfer to a container with a tight seal and store at room temperature for up to 5 days.

WALNUT MYLK BLACK PEPPER DRESSING

Makes ½ cup

¼ cup raw walnuts, soaked 6-8 hours,
    drained, and rinsed

¼ cup water

¼ cup olive oil

1 Tbsp sherry vinegar

1½ tsp lemon juice

½ tsp smoked salt

½ tsp freshly ground black pepper

¼ tsp thyme leaves, minced

3 pinches ground sumac

- In a high-power blender, combine walnuts and water and puree, first on low then gradually raising the speed to high, until creamy.
- Strain the mixture through a nut mylk bag and save the leftover pulp for other snacks and treats (pages 137, 144).
- Whisk the remaining ingredients into the walnut mylk.
- Use immediately or transfer to a glass jar with a tight seal and store in the refrigerator for up to 5 days.

PHAT VITALITY SALAD
WITH PASILLA CHILI BLACK OLIVE DRESSING

PHAT VITALITY SALAD

Serves 2-4

2 large handfuls
    mixed greens

4 radishes, sliced

2 Persian cucumber, sliced

2 small bunches watercress
    leaves

2 small bunches sunflower
    sprouts

1 avocado, sliced

4-inch piece burdock
    (*gobo*) root, peeled and
    julienned

2 green onions, sliced

6 Tbsp raw macadamia
    nuts, chopped

6 Tbsp flat-leaf parsley,
    chopped

4 Tbsp pickled ginger,
    chopped

- In a large serving bowl, add all ingredients and toss until well combined.
- Drizzle with Pasilla Chili Black Olive Dressing and serve.

PASILLA CHILI BLACK OLIVE DRESSING

Makes 1¾ cups

½ cup flaxseed oil

6 Tbsp lemon juice

¼ cup olive oil

¼ cup tamari

3 Tbsp maple syrup

2 Tbsp black olives,
    minced

1 Tbsp ume plum vinegar

1 clove garlic, minced

½ tsp ground pasilla chili

2 pinches ground chipotle

1 dash ground cayenne

- Combine all ingredients in a glass jar, seal, and shake to mix.
- Use immediately or seal and store in the refrigerator for up to 2 weeks.

BURDOCK, OR GOBO, IS NATIVE TO NORTHERN ASIA AND EUROPE, AND POSSESSES NUMEROUS HEALTH BENEFITS. BURDOCK IS A POWERFUL ANTI-INFLAMMATORY AND WORKS TO DETOXIFY THE BLOOD AND INCREASE CIRCULATION, WHICH CORRELATES TO AN IMPROVEMENT IN SKIN CONDITIONS SUCH AS ACNE, ECZEMA, AND PSORIASIS. IT'S BEEN HAILED AS AN APHRODISIAC, AND HAS DEMONSTRATED THE CAPACITY TO INHIBIT THE GROWTH OF CANCEROUS TUMORS, SPECIFICALLY PANCREATIC CARCINOMA. BURDOCK ALSO CONTAINS ANTIOXIDANTS, LIKE QUERCETIN, LUTEOLIN, AND PHENOLIC ACIDS, WHICH PROTECT YOUR CELLS FROM FREE-RADICAL DAMAGE.

BLACK CUMIN ROASTED CAULIFLOWER
WITH TOMATO SALAD & CURRY CRYSTAL FLAKE DRESSING

Serves 4-6

2 heads butter lettuce

1 cup cherry tomatoes, halved

⅓ cup shallot, shaved

½ cup flat-leaf parsley, chopped, for topping

½ cup raw almonds, sliced, for topping

• On individual plates, arrange the lettuce, tomatoes, and shallots, sprinkle with almonds and parsley, top with Black Cumin Roasted Cauliflower slices, and drizzle with Curry Crystal Flake Dressing.

BLACK CUMIN ROASTED CAULIFLOWER

Serves 4-6

1 large head cauliflower, trimmed and sliced into ¼-inch-thick slabs

2-3 Tbsp olive oil

1 Tbsp black cumin seeds

½ tsp sea salt

¼ tsp freshly ground black pepper

¼ tsp smoked paprika

• Preheat oven to 400°F. In a large mixing bowl, combine the cauliflower, oil, black cumin seeds, salt, black pepper, and paprika, and toss until well coated.
• On a baking sheet lined with parchment paper, arrange cauliflower slices and bake, turning once, for about 25 minutes, or until edges are caramelized.

CURRY CRYSTAL FLAKE DRESSING

Makes about ⅔ cup

¼ cup flaxseed oil

2 Tbsp Bragg Liquid Aminos

2 Tbsp lemon juice

1 Tbsp raw honey

2 tsp fresh ginger, finely grated

1 tsp toasted sesame oil

½ tsp E3 AFA Crystal Flakes (or for garnish)

¼ tsp curry powder

⅛ tsp garam masala

2 pinches ground clove

1 pinch chipotle powder

1 pinch ground cumin

• Combine all ingredients in a glass jar, seal, and shake to combine.
• Use immediately or store in the refrigerator for up to 2 weeks.
• For dramatic effect, Crystal Flakes can be sprinkled over the dressed salad as a garnish instead of included in the dressing.

ROASTED FENNEL SALAD

Serves 4

4 large handfuls
   mixed greens
Roasted Fennel
Persian Pickle Salad

Creamy dressing of choice
   (Oaxaca Ranch Dressing,
   Sea Czar Dressing, Miso
   Shiso Cream, or Cashew
   Sumac Yogurt Sauce,
   pages 63, 75, 82, 110)

• On individual plates, arrange mixed greens, top with a few slices of Roasted Fennel, a dollop of Persian Pickle Salad, and drizzle with creamy dressing.

ROASTED FENNEL

Serves 4

4 fennel bulbs, trimmed
   and cut in ½-inch-thick
   slices
4 Tbsp olive oil
3 Tbsp ground raw pine nuts
2 Tbsp ground sesame seeds

2 tsp dried oregano
¾ tsp sea salt
½ tsp freshly ground black
   pepper
¼ cup fennel fronds,
   minced

• Preheat the oven to 400°F. In a medium mixing bowl, combine fennel with oil, pine nuts, sesame seeds, and oregano, season with salt and pepper, and toss well.
• On a baking sheet lined with parchment paper, arrange fennel slices and bake, turning once, for 20-30 minutes, or until the fennel is golden brown and tender when poked with a fork.
• Remove from oven and sprinkle with minced fennel fronds.

PERSIAN PICKLE SALAD

Makes 1½ cups

2 Persian cucumbers, diced
1 Tbsp mint leaves,
   chiffonaded
2 tsp lemon juice
2 tsp white wine vinegar

1 small clove garlic, minced
½ tsp salt
1 pinch pink peppercorns,
   crushed
1 pinch dried dill

• In a mixing bowl, add all ingredients and toss well to combine.
• Use immediately or store in a tightly sealed container in the refrigerator for up to 2 days.

SEA CZAR SALAD
WITH SEA CZAR DRESSING

Serves 2-4

1 head romaine lettuce, chopped

12 cherry tomatoes, halved

2 big handfuls kale leaves, destemmed and torn into bite-size pieces

1½ cups Feisty Breadcrumbs (page 66)

6 Tbsp flat-leaf parsley, minced

3 Tbsp shallot, thinly sliced

¼ cup Sea Czar Dressing

Freshly ground black pepper

Lemon zest, for garnish

• In a large salad bowl, combine lettuce, tomatoes, kale, Feisty Breadcrumbs, parsley, and shallot.

• Drizzle with Sea Czar Dressing, season with black pepper, and toss until well combined. Garnish with lemon zest.

SEA CZAR DRESSING

Makes 1½ cups

2½ cups water

3 Tbsp raw pine nuts

2 Tbsp raw macadamia nuts

2 Tbsp raw cashews

1 pinch dried wakame

1 small clove garlic, minced

1 Tbsp tamarind paste

1 Tbsp lemon juice

2 Tbsp white wine vinegar

1 tsp Dijon mustard

½ tsp salt

½ tsp unpasteurized white miso

¼ tsp freshly ground black pepper

¼ cup olive oil

• In a medium bowl, place all nuts and wakame with 2 cups water, and soak overnight. Drain and rinse.

• In a high-power blender, place drained soaked nuts and wakame with the remaining ingredients, including ½ cup water, and puree, first on low then gradually raising the speed to high, until well mixed.

• Use immediately or transfer to a glass jar with a tight seal and store in the refrigerator for up to 5 days.

MIZUNA NIÇOISE
WITH UME BALSAMIC VINAIGRETTE

Serves 2-4

2-3 cups mizuna (Japanese mustard greens)

2-3 Tbsp Ume Balsamic Vinaigrette, plus more as desired

8 cherry tomatoes, halved

2 radishes, sliced

4 small red potatoes, boiled and cubed, or 2 whole large hard-boiled eggs, quartered

1 Persian cucumber, sliced

16 haricots verts, blanched

1 avocado, sliced

8 Kalamata olives, pitted

4 pieces okra, thinly sliced

1 small shallot, sliced

1 small bunch watercress leaves, for garnish

1 Tbsp flat-leaf parsley, minced, for garnish

Freshly ground black pepper

- In a large serving bowl, lightly dress the mizuna with the Ume Balsamic Vinaigrette. Adorn with tomatoes, radishes, potato cubes or egg quarters, cucumber, haricots verts, avocado, olives, okra, and shallot in small bunches.
- Garnish with parsley and watercress, season with black pepper. Drizzle with more dressing, if desired.

FOR IMPROVED FOOD COMBINING AND DIGESTION, MAKE THIS SALAD WITH EITHER THE PROTEIN (EGG) OR THE STARCH (POTATOES).

UME BALSAMIC VINAIGRETTE

Makes 1 cup

5 Tbsp olive oil

3 Tbsp balsamic vinegar

3 Tbsp flaxseed oil

2 Tbsp lemon juice

1 Tbsp Dijon mustard

2 tsp umeboshi paste

1½ tsp maple syrup

1 tsp white pepper

½ tsp salt

2 pinches freshly ground black pepper

1-2 Tbsp water, as needed, for thinning

- In a glass jar, combine all ingredients except the water. Seal tightly and shake to combine. If desired, thin the dressing with a little water as needed and shake again.
- Use immediately or store in the refrigerator for up to 1 week.

PARSNIP OF THE SEA SALAD

This versatile dish can be used as a topping for a green salad, as a sandwich base, as a spread on crackers, or even as an alternative filling for That's a Collard Wrap, page 84.

Makes 1½ cups

3½ oz parsnip, peeled

2 oz burdock (*gobo*) root, peeled

2 Tbsp water

1 pinch wakame seaweed

1 oz celery, diced

1 Tbsp flat-leaf parsley, minced

1 Tbsp shallot, minced

2 tsp flaxseed oil

2 tsp dried dill weed

¾ tsp smoked salt

1 dash smoked paprika

2 Tbsp raw tahini

1½ Tbsp lemon juice

- Using a grater, mandoline, or a food processor with a very fine shredding blade, shred the parsnip and burdock root into a large serving bowl. (Don't worry if the burdock turns brown, as it will lighten when the lemon juice is added.)
- In a small mixing bowl, combine water and wakame and set aside to soak for 30 minutes, or until it moistens and unfolds.
- Pour the wakame soaking water into the bowl with the parsnips and burdock. Mince the wakame into small pieces and add it as well. Add the celery, parsley, shallot, oil, dill, salt, and paprika and toss to combine.
- In a small mixing bowl, whisk together the tahini and lemon juice until creamy. Fold the dressing into the salad and serve.

A BROWN SEA VEGETABLE, WAKAME IS DENSELY LOADED WITH VITAMINS AND MINERALS SUCH AS BIOAVAILABLE IODINE, ESSENTIAL FOR MAINTAINING THYROID HEALTH. WAKAME ALSO CONTAINS A COMPOUND CALLED FUCOXANTHIN, WHICH PROMOTES WEIGHT LOSS. FURTHERMORE, WAKAME HAS BEEN SHOWN TO HAVE ANTICANCER PROPERTIES FOR LEUKEMIA AS WELL AS LUNG, BREAST, AND PROSTATE CANCERS. IN ADDITION, WAKAME, LIKE OTHER BROWN SEAWEEDS, IS RICH IN SODIUM ALGINATE, WHICH HAS BEEN SHOWN TO BIND WITH STRONTIUM AND HELP NEUTRALIZE RADIATION POISONING.

FINE & MELLOW KRAUT

Enjoy the probiotic benefits of fresh sauerkraut without the potency of fully fermented flavor.

FERMENTED FOODS SUCH AS UNPASTEURIZED SAUER-KRAUT, KIMCHI, YOGURT, KEFIR, MISO, AND KOMBUCHA CONTAIN BENEFICIAL PROBIOTIC CULTURES THAT DIRECTLY AFFECT MOOD, DIGESTIVE HEALTH, AND THE IMMUNE SYSTEM. UPWARDS OF 90 PERCENT OF THE SEROTONIN USED BY THE BODY IS MANUFACTURED BY PROBIOTIC CULTURES IN THE GUT, RELAYED UP THE VAGUS NERVE TO SUPPLY THE BRAIN, IMPACTING EVERY PART OF THE BODY FROM EMOTIONS TO MOTOR SKILLS TO THE WILL TO PRESS ON IN THE FACE OF STRESS AND LIFE CHALLENGES. THIS IMPORTANT MOOD-STABILIZING NEUROTRANSMITTER REDUCES DEPRESSION AND REGULATES ANXIETY WHILE ALSO HELPING TO REGULATE SLEEP CYCLES, DIGESTION, AND APPETITE. ADD A SPOONFUL OF KRAUT TO EVERY MEAL, TO HELP REPLENISH PROBIOTIC RANKS WITH A MINIMUM OF 10 BILLION CFUs (COLONY-FORMING UNITS) EVERY DAY.

Makes 1 quart

1 head white or green cabbage, shredded thinly

⅓ cup fermented red cabbage or beet sauerkraut (such as from Wildbrine, Farmhouse Culture, or Rejuvenative Foods)

2 Tbsp lemon juice

2 Tbsp shallot, shaved

1½ tsp caraway seeds

½–1 tsp salt

Water, as needed

• In a large mixing bowl, combine shredded fresh cabbage, fermented cabbage, lemon juice, shallot, and caraway seeds. Season with salt and toss until well combined.

• Pack firmly into 2 pint jars or 1 quart jar, add enough water to completely cover the sauerkraut, and seal.

• Store on top of refrigerator for 12-24 hours, then transfer to the refrigerator and store for up to 10 days.

4

ROLLS, WRAPS
& TAPAS

HERBACEOUS SUMMER ROLLS
WITH SESAME ALMOND SAUCE & MISO SHISO CREAM

Serves 2-4, makes 10-15 rolls

Hot water, as needed

10-15 sheets rice paper
(*or* fresh collard leaves)

10-15 leaves fresh cilantro

10-15 leaves fresh basil

10-15 leaves fresh mint

½ head white cabbage,
shaved

2 avocados, sliced
very thinly

2 Persian cucumbers,
thickly julienned

1 large carrot, peeled and
cut into matchsticks

1 handful radish sprouts

Sesame Almond Sauce
and Miso Shiso Cream,
for dipping

Baby lettuce and
Fine & Mellow Kraut
(page 79), for serving
(optional)

A NUMBER OF OTHER DRESSINGS OR SAUCES WOULD ALSO GO WELL, SUCH AS MELLOW WASABI DRESSING (PAGE 184), BLACK GARLIC TAMARIND SAUCE (PAGE 90), CARROT ZIP-ZAP DRESSING (PAGE 184), OR GOJI-TOMATO CHILI PASTE (PAGE 173) FOR A SPICY KICK.

- Place a large, shallow pan filled with hot water over the lowest possible heat to just keep warm.
- Place a sheet of rice paper in the hot water to soften, remove as soon as it becomes pliable, and transfer to a moistened cutting board to prevent sticking.
- Assemble the roll by first laying down 1 leaf of each herb, so they can be seen through the wrapper. Then cover the herbs with a few shreds of cabbage, add slices of avocado, cucumber, a large pinch of carrot, and a few radish sprouts.
- Carefully roll up the bundle, folding in the sides like a burrito.
- Repeat with the remaining sheets of rice paper until all ingredients have been used.
- Rolls may be sliced in half crosswise or left whole, served with the Sesame Almond Sauce and Miso Shiso Cream for dipping, and with baby lettuce and Fine & Mellow Kraut, if desired.

SESAME ALMOND SAUCE

Makes 1¾ cups

½ cup almond butter

½ roma tomato

⅓ cup water

2 Tbsp tamari

2 Tbsp lemon juice

1½ Tbsp raw honey

1 Tbsp flaxseed oil

1 Tbsp ume plum vinegar

½ tsp hot sesame oil

¼ tsp mustard powder

¼ tsp white pepper

2 pinches chili flakes

- In a high-power blender, combine all ingredients and puree, first on low then gradually raising the speed to high, until smooth and creamy.
- Use immediately or transfer to a glass jar with a tight seal and store in the refrigerator for up to 1 week.

MISO SHISO CREAM

Makes 1½ cups

15-18 whole shiso leaves,
    green or purple
⅔ cup raw cashews,
    soaked 4-6 hours,
    drained, and rinsed
½ cup water
3 Tbsp ume plum vinegar

2 Tbsp olive oil
2 Tbsp lemon juice
1 Tbsp unpasteurized
    white miso
1 Tbsp flaxseed oil
¼ tsp sea salt
¼ tsp white pepper

• In a high-power blender, combine all ingredients and puree, first on low then gradually raising the speed to high, until smooth and creamy.

• Use immediately or transfer to a glass jar with a tight seal and store in the refrigerator for up to 5 days.

SHISO IS A MEMBER OF THE MINT FAMILY, WITH STRONG ANTIMICROBIAL AND ANTI-INFLAMMATORY PROPERTIES. IT ALSO REMEDIES A NUMBER OF DIGESTIVE ISSUES, FROM NAUSEA AND MORNING SICKNESS TO CONSTIPATION. DUE TO THE RELATIONSHIP BETWEEN THE INTESTINES AND THE LUNGS, SHISO ALSO TREATS COLDS, FLU, AND OTHER RESPIRATORY TRACT INFECTIONS, AND IT IS EVEN BELIEVED TO HELP ALLEVIATE ALLERGIES IF CONSUMED REGULARLY.

THAT'S A COLLARD WRAP

Serves 1-2

1-2 collard leaves

⅓ cup Macadamia Ricotta
(page 182)

½ Persian cucumber, sliced

½ avocado, sliced

1 small tomato, sliced

1 large handful mixed
greens

1 small handful sprouts

2 Tbsp unpasteurized
sauerkraut (or Fine &
Mellow Kraut, page 79)

2-3 Tbsp Mellow Wasabi
Dressing (page 184),
Carrot Zip-Zap
Dressing (page 184), or
Chimichurri (page 179)

• Cut collard leaves in half along stems.
Overlap them to create a circular wrap,
if desired.

• Layer on the Macadamia Ricotta,
cucumber, avocado, tomato, mixed
greens, sprouts, and sauerkraut.

• Drizzle with the condiment of choice,
and roll up the bundle, folding in the
sides like a burrito.

COLLARD GREENS ARE UNSUNG HEROES IN THE PANTHEON OF CANCER-FIGHTING CRUCIFEROUS BRASSICAS. KALE AND BROCCOLI USUALLY HOG THE LIMELIGHT WHILE THE HUMBLE COLLARD IS WORKING BACKSTAGE, LESS EXPENSIVE AND MILDER IN TASTE. IN TERMS OF ANTIOXIDANT-RICH CANCER-FIGHTING FOODS, CRUCIFEROUS VEGETABLES TOP THE LIST DUE TO SULFUR COMPOUNDS CALLED GLUCOSINOLATES, ACTIVATED WHEN THE LEAVES ARE CUT OR CHEWED. COLLARDS, LIKE OTHER BRASSICAS, ARE ANTI-INFLAMMATORY AND LOADED WITH VITAMINS A, B, C, E & K; CALCIUM, CHOLINE, COPPER, MANGANESE, PHOSPHORUS, POTASSIUM, AND OMEGA-3s. WHEN IT COMES TO BOOSTING LIVER FUNCTION AND AIDING THE BLOOD-DETOX PROCESS, CRUCIFEROUS VEGGIES ARE ALL-AROUND ROCK STARS, BUT THE FIBERS IN COLLARDS HAVE THE DISTINCTION OF BINDING MORE EFFECTIVELY WITH USED BILE IN THE GUT THAN ANY OTHER BRASSICA. THIS IS GOOD NEWS: THE LIVER STORES THE TOXINS THAT IT PULLS FROM THE BLOODSTREAM IN BILE, TOXIN-LADEN BILE BINDS WITH FIBER IN THE GUT, AND IS ELIMINATED FROM THE BODY. THIS FORCES THE LIVER TO MAKE FRESH BILE, PULLING MORE TOXINS AND CHOLESTEROL OUT OF THE BLOODSTREAM. NATURALLY, THIS LOWERS CHOLESTEROL, REDUCES TOXIN LOAD, IMPROVES DIGESTION, AND THWARTS A NUMBER OF CANCERS.

TRAMPO

Makes 2 cups, serves 2-4

3 roma tomatoes, diced

½ cup green bell pepper,
diced

⅓ cup diced onion

3 Tbsp olive oil

2 Tbsp flat-leaf parsley,
minced

½ tsp salt

• In a medium serving bowl, toss all
ingredients and until well combined.

• This is excellent served with
the Calabaza Tortilla (page 31) or
as a summertime dish alongside
Pa Amb Oli (page 88).

84

JING TIME RICE NORI ROLLS
WITH WAKAME MISO SOUP

Makes 5 rolls

3½ cups freshly cooked Jing Time
   Rice (page 106)

3 Tbsp Sushi Vinegar

5 sheets toasted nori seaweed

10 fresh shiso leaves

3 leaves lacinato kale, quartered
   and de-stemmed

1 large carrot, finely julienned

1 handful radish sprouts

1-2 avocados, sliced thinly

1 Persian cucumber, deseeded and
   julienned into thick strips

2-3 Tbsp umeboshi paste

1 small bowl water, room
   temperature, to seal rolls

Citrus Ponzu (page 96), for dipping

• In a large, flat-bottom wooden bowl, place the hot Jing Time
Rice. Pour the Sushi Vinegar over the rice. Using a rice paddle,
cut and flip the rice to distribute the vinegar, while fanning the
rice to disperse the steam. Continue until the rice has cooled
somewhat but remains slightly warm.

• Lay 1 sheet of nori on a rolling mat with the shiny side down
and the lines pointing straight ahead. Spread ⅔ cup Jing Time
Rice on the lower half of the nori sheet, forming a neat, even
rectangle spreading out to the left and right edges. Layer
on 2 shiso leaves, then some kale, carrot, and radish sprouts
(arrange these so the tops will poke out of the roll's ends).
Last, add some of the avocado and cucumber, and wipe a small
amount of umeboshi paste over the cucumber. Try to keep the
vegetables centered in the middle of the rice.

• To roll, use the mat to fold the rice over the vegetables
(as if you are going to fold the nori into fourths, starting with
the bottom half). Once the rice is tucked end to end, continue
to roll up the rice inside the remaining nori using the mat.
At the edge, dip a finger in water and run it along the edge
to make it sticky and seal the roll.

• Repeat with the remaining nori sheets until all the
ingredients have been used.

• Cut each roll into 5-6 even slices. Serve with the Wakame
Miso Soup and with the Citrus Ponzu as a dipping sauce.

SUSHI VINEGAR

Makes 3 Tbsp

2 Tbsp rice vinegar

1 Tbsp raw honey

½ tsp salt

• Combine all ingredients in a glass jar with a tight seal and
shake until the honey is dissolved. Use immediately or store
in the refrigerator for up to 1 week.

WAKAME MISO SOUP

Serves 4-6

½ cup water

⅓ cup dried wakame seaweed

4 cups Kombu Dashi (page 47)

3 Tbsp unpasteurized white miso

1-2 green onions, sliced thinly,
   for garnish

- In a small bowl, combine water and wakame and set aside for 30 minutes, or until softened. Drain and rinse.
- In a medium pot over low heat, warm 1 cup of Kombu Dashi. Stir in the miso, add the wakame and the remaining 3 cups of Kombu Dashi, and warm until the soup is just hot.
- Remove from heat, garnish with green onion slices, and serve.

IN CHINESE MEDICINE, JING IS THE FUNDAMENTAL CHARGE IN ONE'S BEING. THE ENERGY NEEDED FOR LIVING, JING DRAINS AWAY A LITTLE BIT EVERY DAY, BUT STRESS, CAFFEINE, LACK OF SLEEP, HEAVY DRINKING, DISEASE, TRAUMATIC INJURY, ROUGH SPORTS, AND EMOTIONAL CRISIS CAN ALSO DRAIN IT. ADAPTOGENS (E.G., ASHWAGANDA, ASTRAGALUS, CHAGA, GINSENG, REISHI, RHODIOLA, SCHIZANDRA) CAN HELP MITIGATE THE EFFECTS OF STRESS AND CERTAIN FOODS ALSO HELP REBUILD JING, INCLUDING ADUKI BEANS, BLACK BEANS, BLACK RICE, MISO, NATTO, TEMPEH, CULTURED VEGETABLES, SEA VEGETABLES, SPIRULINA, PINE POLLEN, BEE POLLEN, ROYAL JELLY, DARK GREEN LEAFY VEGGIES, BONE BROTH, WALNUTS, SESAME, ARTICHOKES, AND WATERCRESS—AS WELL AS LAUGHTER, DANCING, MASSAGE, EXERCISE, AND LISTENING TO MUSIC.

PA AMB OLI

Simply translated, "bread and oil" is a staple of Mallorcan cuisine dating back to the eighteenth century. Served as a tapa for breakfast, lunch, or dinner, Pa Amb Oli was developed to bring new life to dry bread, by moistening it with small ramallet tomatoes and drizzling with olive oil. Explore the endless possibilities of this satisfyingly delicious simple dish: Try topping it with garnishes such as grilled or caramelized onions, roasted red peppers, sliced green onions, a dollop of Macadamia Ricotta, rock samphire, green olives, or seasonal figs and prickly pears.

Serves 2-4

¼ cup olive oil

½ red onion, thinly sliced

Salt and freshly ground
   black pepper

Splash sherry vinegar

2-4 thin slices sprouted
   sourdough or other
   brown bread, toasted

1-2 cloves garlic,
   finely minced

6-8 cluster tomatoes,
   halved

SUGGESTED GARNISHES

½ cup sliced or whole
   Spanish olives

⅓ cup roasted red
   bell pepper

1 handful rock samphire,
   purslane, or watercress
   leaves

2-3 Tbsp Macadamia
   Ricotta (page 182)

1 green onion, sliced
   thinly

• In a small skillet over low heat, warm 2 Tbsp olive oil. Add onion, season with salt, black pepper, and sherry vinegar, and sauté, tossing occasionally, for 10-15 minutes, or until lightly caramelized. Remove from heat and set aside.

• Rub toast slices with garlic, if desired, and smear them with the insides of the tomatoes. Season with salt and drizzle remaining oil over the bread.

• Serve with garnishes as desired.

ADDING A FRESH LEAFY TOPPING TO BREAD IMPROVES ITS DIGESTION. LONG USED TO TREAT DISEASE AND BELIEVED TO PURIFY THE BLOOD, WATERCRESS IS LOADED WITH CALCIUM, IRON, MANGANESE, VITAMINS A, C & K, WHICH FORTIFIES THE BONES AND CAN PREVENT NEURONAL DAMAGE IN THE BRAIN. WATERCRESS HAS ANTICANCER PROPERTIES, DUE TO PHYTONUTRIENTS AND ANTIOXIDANTS, SPECIFICALLY THE PEPPERY-TASTING GLUCONASTURTIIN, A SOURCE OF PHENETHYL ISOTHIOCYANATES (PEITC), A COMPOUND THAT STUDIES HAVE FOUND TO INHIBIT TUMOR GROWTH. PURSLANE HAS A SALTY/SOUR FLAVOR AND CONTAINS OMEGA-3s. WITH COPIOUS AMOUNTS OF CALCIUM, IRON, MAGNESIUM, MANGANESE, POTASSIUM, A & B VITAMINS, AND PHYTONUTRIENTS AND ANTIOXIDANTS SUCH AS BETALAIN AND CAROTENOIDS, PURSLANE HELPS WARD OFF CANCER AND SUPPLY THE NUTRITION TO FEEL FULL AFTER A MEAL. ALSO KNOWN AS SAMPHIRE OR SEA FENNEL, ROCK SAMPHIRE GROWS ALONG THE ATLANTIC SHORES IN BRITAIN, EUROPE, NORWAY, AND THE MEDITERRANEAN. EATEN FRESH OR STEAMED, SAMPHIRE IS HIGH IN VITAMIN C, IRON, MAGNESIUM, ZINC, AND BIOAVAILABLE IODINE; HAS ANTI-INFLAMMATORY, DIURETIC, AND ANTIMICROBIAL PROPERTIES; AND IS THOUGHT TO TREAT OBESITY (IODINE BENEFITS A SLUGGISH THYROID). DUE TO THE PRESENCE OF FUROCOUMARINS, SOME PEOPLE ARE MORE SENSITIVE TO SUNLIGHT AFTER CONSUMING IT.

PAD THAI SLAW LETTUCE WRAPS
WITH BLACK GARLIC TAMARIND SAUCE, THAI TEMPEH & HONEY CHILI SAUCE

For this recipe, be sure to make the Black Garlic Tamarind Sauce first! It can be made with tamarind paste to save time, but for a memorable, earthy, slow-food experience, start with whole tamarind pods. As a rule of thumb, 3-4 lettuce wraps per person makes an excellent light meal.

BLACK GARLIC TAMARIND SAUCE

Serves 2-4

2½ oz tamarind pods, shelled, seeded, and stemmed, *or* 2 Tbsp tamarind paste

2¾ oz water, plus more as needed

½ oz fresh ginger, peeled and chopped

½ oz olive oil

½ oz tamari

½ oz coconut syrup

2 cloves black garlic

¾ tsp ume plum vinegar

• Crack open the tamarind pods. Remove the veins and pluck out the shiny black seeds from the fleshy fruit. Discard only the pod shells, veins, and black seeds; be sure to retain the sticky seed casings.

• In a high-power blender, combine all ingredients and puree, first on low then gradually raising the speed to high, until smooth, adding a little more water to thin, if necessary.

• Use immediately or transfer to a squeeze bottle or a glass jar with a tight seal and store in the refrigerator for up to 2 weeks.

HONEY CHILI SAUCE

2 Tbsp raw honey

2 Tbsp ume plum vinegar

1 tsp hot sesame oil

2 pinches red chili flakes

• Combine all ingredients in a glass jar with a tight seal, and shake until a syrupy sauce forms.

• Use immediately or store in the refrigerator for up to 1 week.

PAD THAI SLAW

½ small green cabbage head, shaved

1 carrot, julienned

3 green onions, sliced in thin rounds

5 Tbsp Black Garlic Tamarind Sauce

2 Tbsp fresh cilantro, chopped

2 Tbsp raw macadamia nuts,
   chopped

• In a large mixing bowl, combine all ingredients and toss until mixture is evenly coated and relaxes into a slaw.

THAI TEMPEH

8 oz tempeh, cut into small cubes

½ cup shallots, chopped

¼ cup tamari

2 Tbsp mirin

2 tsp sesame oil

2 tsp coconut oil

½ tsp red chili flakes

¼ tsp freshly ground black pepper

• In a small bowl, combine the tempeh, shallots, tamari, mirin, and sesame oil. Set aside to marinate for 15-20 minutes.

• In a medium skillet over low heat, warm the coconut oil. Add contents of the bowl to the skillet and gently simmer, stirring occasionally, for 10-12 minutes, or until the liquid disappears and everything is nicely golden brown and sticky.

SERVING & GARNISH

1 head butter lettuce,
   leaves separated

Lime wedges, for garnish

• Arrange butter lettuce leaves on individual plates, add a scoop of Pad Thai Slaw and a dollop of hot Thai Tempeh on each leaf. Serve with Honey Chili Sauce to drizzle over the wraps and garnish with lime wedges.

THE SUPER MOLÉ

Serves 2-4

2 avocados, cubed

1 tomato, diced

1 ear corn kernels

½ cup celery, diced

3 Tbsp red onion, diced

3 Tbsp cilantro, minced

3 Tbsp lime juice

1 Tbsp flat-leaf parsley, chopped

1 Tbsp flaxseed oil

1 tsp ginger, finely grated

½ tsp sea salt

3 pinches ground cumin

3 dashes chipotle powder

1 head romaine or butter lettuce, leaves separated

3 cucumbers, cut in wedges, for serving

½ cup marcona almonds, chopped, for garnish

1 tsp E3Live AFA Crystal Flakes, for garnish

2-4 Tbsp Pasilla Chili Black Olive Dressing (page 68)

• In a large serving bowl, gently toss together the avocados, tomato, corn, celery, onion, cilantro, lime juice, parsley, oil, ginger, salt, cumin, and chipotle.

• Serve over lettuce leaves, top with cucumber wedges, sprinkle with almonds and E3Live AFA Crystal Flakes, and drizzle with Pasilla Chili Black Olive Dressing.

LOVE YOUR ROOTS NORI ROLLS

Serves 2-4

LOVE YOUR ROOTS SALAD

2 carrots, peeled and shredded fine

1 small yam, peeled and shredded fine

2 Tbsp almond butter

2 Tbsp lemon juice

1 Tbsp tamari

1 tsp unpasteurized white miso

½ cup celery, diced

3 Tbsp shallot, minced

2 Tbsp cilantro, minced

1½ Tbsp ginger, minced

1 Tbsp flat-leaf parsley, minced

1 tsp nutritional yeast

NORI HANDROLLS

4 sheets nori seaweed, cut in half

1 Persian cucumber, julienned

1-2 avocados, sliced

2 handfuls mixed baby greens

20 radish or buckwheat sprouts

4-inch piece burdock (gobo) root, peeled and julienned

¼ cup pickled ginger

Love Your Roots Salad

Citrus Ponzu (page 96), for dipping

• In a large serving bowl, place the finely shredded carrots and yam.

• In a small bowl, combine almond butter, lemon juice, tamari, and miso and whisk until well combined.

• Pour almond butter mixture over the shredded carrots and yam. Fold in the celery, shallot, cilantro, ginger, parsley, and nutritional yeast.

• Divide and stack the cucumber, avocado, mixed baby greens, sprouts, burdock, and pickled ginger, along with the Love Your Roots Salad, over two half sheets of nori, making sure the leafy tops of the lettuce and sprouts are peeking out of the edge. Roll up into a fancy cone or a little burrito.

• Repeat with the remaining nori sheets until all ingredients have been used.

• Serve with Citrus Ponzu for dipping.

QUINOA WAKAME CROQUETTE NORI ROLLS
WITH CHILI GINGER MACADAMIA CREAM, RED PEPPER RELISH & CITRUS PONZU

QUINOA WAKAME CROQUETTES

Makes 20 croquettes, serves 4

1½ cups + 2 Tbsp water

½ cup dry quinoa

12 oz butternut squash, cubed

3 oz yam, cubed

2 oz red onion, diced

3½-4 Tbsp coconut oil

1 tsp sea salt

¼ tsp freshly ground black pepper

¼ tsp chipotle powder

⅙ oz dried wakame seaweed,
    soaked for 10 minutes, drained,
    and chopped

⅞ oz kale, finely chopped

⅞ oz celery, finely chopped

½ oz flat-leaf parsley, minced

3 Tbsp ground chia seeds

• Preheat oven to 425°F. In a pot over high heat, combine 1½ cups water and quinoa and bring to a boil.

• Reduce heat to low and cook for about 15 minutes, or until water is absorbed and the bottom of the grains begins to crackle. Remove from heat, cover, and set aside.

• In a medium mixing bowl, combine the squash, yam, onion, 2 Tbsp coconut oil, ½ tsp salt, black pepper, and chipotle powder and toss until well coated.

• On a baking sheet lined with parchment paper, spread the vegetables in an even layer and roast for 20 minutes. Remove from oven and set aside, leaving oven on to bake the croquettes.

• While vegetables are roasting, in a large mixing bowl, add wakame, kale, celery, parsley, chia seeds, remaining 1½-2 Tbsp coconut oil, and remaining ½ tsp salt, and toss until well combined. Add the cooked quinoa and roasted vegetables and gently mash everything together. Moisten the mixture with the remaining 2 Tbsp water.

• Form the mixture into croquettes, either 3-inch logs, or ovals or balls about 1 inch in diameter. On a baking sheet lined with parchment paper, lay out the croquettes and bake for 15 minutes on each side, or until lightly browned. Remove from oven.

• Use immediately or make ahead of time and reheat later. If storing, wrap with wax paper between each croquette and secure in plastic wrap or bags. Store in the refrigerator for up to 5-7 days.

94

RECIPE CONTINUES ⟶

RED PEPPER RELISH

Makes 1½ cups, serves 4-8 as a condiment

2 small red bell peppers, cut into chunks

½ red onion, cut into chunks

2 small cloves garlic, minced

2 Tbsp lemon juice

2 Tbsp flaxseed oil

2 tsp smoked paprika

½ tsp salt

- In a food processor, combine all ingredients and pulse, periodically scraping down the sides, until the mixture becomes a juicy relish.
- Use immediately or transfer to a glass jar with a tight seal and store in the refrigerator for up to 3-5 days.

CHILI GINGER MACADAMIA CREAM

Makes about 2 cups, serves 6-10 as a condiment

½ cup raw macadamia nuts, soaked overnight, drained, and rinsed

½ cup water

¼ cup raw pine nuts, soaked overnight, drained, and rinsed

1 oz ginger, peeled and sliced

3½ Tbsp lemon juice

1 Tbsp flaxseed oil

2 tsp raw honey

2 tsp Bragg Liquid Aminos *or* unpasteurized white miso

1 tsp coconut oil

½ tsp smoked sea salt

½ tsp hot sesame oil

¼-½ tsp chili flakes

- In a high-power blender, combine all ingredients and puree, first on low then gradually raising the speed to high, until smooth and creamy.
- Use immediately or transfer to a glass jar with a tight seal and store in the refrigerator for up to 5-7 days.

PINE NUTS CONTAIN HEALTHY FATS THAT STIMULATE THE RELEASE OF CHOLECYSTOKININ (CCK), A HORMONE THAT SUPPRESSES THE APPETITE. THEY ARE ALSO A RICH SOURCE OF METHYL-SULFONYLMETHANE (MSM), A BIOAVAILABLE FORM OF SULFUR THAT SUPPORTS JOINT AND SKIN HEALTH. BECAUSE THE LIVER EMPLOYS SULFUR TO BIND TOXINS INTO BILE, SULFUR COMPOUNDS HELP TO DETOXIFY THE BLOODSTREAM AND RESOLVE INFLAMMATION. MSM IS ONE OF THE BUILDING BLOCKS OF GLUTATHIONE, WHICH DEFENDS THE MITOCHONDRIAL ENGINES OF THE CELLS AND CAN ALSO RESUSCITATE OTHER ANTIOXIDANTS.

CITRUS PONZU

Makes about ⅔ cup

3 Tbsp Bragg Liquid Aminos

3 Tbsp water

2 Tbsp lemon juice

2 Tbsp rice vinegar

1 Tbsp orange juice

- Combine all ingredients in a glass jar, seal tightly, and shake to mix.
- Use immediately or store in the refrigerator for up to 1 week.

NORi HANDROLLS ASSEMBLY & SERViNG

Serves 4

4 sheets nori seaweed,
   cut in half
8 Quinoa Wakame
   Croquettes, warmed
2 handfuls baby greens
1 large handful buckwheat
   sprouts, trimmed
4-inch piece cucumber,
   seeded and julienned
2 avocados, quartered

Chili Ginger Macadamia
   Cream
Red Pepper Relish
Small bowl water,
   for sealing nori edges
Citrus Ponzu, for dipping
Mixed green salad tossed
   with Basil Oil Dressing
   (page 166), for serving

• To assemble, lay down a halved nori sheet horizontally. On one side, stack a Quinoa Wakame Croquette and a pinch each of the baby greens, sprouts, and cucumber, ¼ avocado, and spoonfuls of the Chili Ginger Macadamia Cream and Red Pepper Relish. Wrap the nori to form a cone. At the edge, dip a finger in water and run it along the edge to make it sticky and seal the roll.

• Repeat with the remaining nori sheets until all ingredients have been used.

• Serve wraps with Citrus Ponzu for a dipping sauce and with a mixed green salad tossed with Basil Oil Dressing.

5
GRAINS & MAINS

ANCHO-ROASTED SQUASH
OVER GREENS WITH FERMENTED TOMATILLO SALSA & SMOKY PINE NUT CREAM

ANCHO-ROASTED SQUASH

Serves 4-6

3 cups butternut squash, cubed

3 cups summer squash, cubed

½ cup red onion, diced

3 Tbsp olive oil

2 cloves garlic, minced

¾ tsp sea salt

1-2 tsp dried ground ancho chili

Freshly ground black pepper

4-6 handfuls baby lettuces or mixed greens

½ cup pumpkin seeds, toasted, for garnish

- Preheat the oven to 400°F. In a mixing bowl, combine the squash, onion, oil, garlic, ancho chili, and salt. Season with black pepper and toss until well coated.
- Transfer to a baking sheet lined with parchment paper and roast for 25 minutes.
- On individual plates, arrange greens and top with Ancho-Roasted Squash and dollops of Fermented Tomatillo Salsa and Smoky Pine Nut Cream. Garnish with toasted pumpkin seeds.

FERMENTED TOMATILLO SALSA

Makes 2¼ cups

1¾ cups tomatillos, peeled, washed, and chopped

2 Tbsp spicy cultured vegetables (kimchi or other spicy fermented preparation)

¼ cup fresh cilantro, coarsely chopped

3 Tbsp lime juice

2 Tbsp onion, minced

1 tsp jalapeño pepper, minced

½ tsp sea salt

- In a food processor, combine the tomatillos and cultured vegetables and pulse into a slush. Add remaining ingredients and pulse a few times until well mixed.
- Use immediately or transfer to a glass jar with a tight seal and store in the refrigerator for 3 days, or longer, for extra fermented flavor.

SMOKY PINE NUT CREAM

Makes 1¼ cups

¼ cup raw pine nuts, soaked 2-3 hours, drained, and rinsed

1-inch piece chipotle pepper

6 sundried tomato halves

¾ cup warm water

2 Tbsp lemon juice

2 Tbsp flaxseed oil

1 Tbsp almond butter

2 tsp raw honey

2 tsp Bragg Liquid Aminos

1 tsp smoked paprika

½ tsp salt

- In a small mixing bowl, soak the chipotle pepper and sundried tomatoes in the warm water for 15-30 minutes.
- In a high-power blender, combine all ingredients, including the soaking water, and puree, first on low then gradually raising the speed to high, until smooth and creamy.
- Use immediately or transfer to a glass jar with a tight seal and store in the refrigerator for up to 1 week.

BELUGA LENTIL SALAD
WITH JERUSALEM ARTICHOKE

Serves 4-6

2 cups beluga lentils

2½ cups lightly salted water

9 cherry tomatoes, halved

3 small Jerusalem
 artichokes, thinly sliced

¼ cup flat-leaf parsley,
 coarsely chopped

⅓ cup celery *or* fennel,
 minced

1½ oz red onion, shaved

2 Tbsp mint leaves, torn

2 Tbsp flaxseed oil

2 Tbsp lemon juice

1 Tbsp olive oil

1 Tbsp red wine vinegar

1 clove black garlic, minced

½ tsp salt

¼ tsp freshly ground
 black pepper

4 dashes smoked paprika

• In a pot over high heat, bring the water to a boil. Add the lentils, reduce heat to low, and simmer for 25-30 minutes, or until the water is absorbed and the lentils are soft.

• Transfer lentils to a serving bowl and add the remaining ingredients. Toss gently to combine.

• This dish can be served warm or chilled.

WOODSMOKE SHIITAKE MUSHROOMS

Serves 4-6

2 Tbsp olive oil

⅔ cup shallot, thinly sliced

3 cloves garlic, minced

1 tsp rosemary leaves,
 minced

2 cups shiitake
 mushrooms, sliced

3 pinches smoked sea salt

3 dashes chipotle powder

3 dashes ume plum vinegar

3 dashes tamari

Freshly ground black
 pepper

• In a skillet over medium heat, warm the oil. Add shallot, garlic, and rosemary and cook, stirring a few times, for 5 minutes.

• Add the mushrooms and sauté for a just over 1 minute. Stir in the salt, chipotle, vinegar, tamari, and black pepper.

• Serve hot, perhaps over Truffle Hunter's Wild Rice (page 122), as an added accompaniment to the Daikon Nimono meal (page 106), or as a stand-in for tempeh in the Pad Thai Lettuce Wraps (page 90).

MUSHROOMS ABSORB WHATEVER IS IN THE SOIL, SO BE SURE TO GET ORGANICALLY GROWN TO AVOID INGESTING TOXINS. TO REAP THE FULL PROTECTIVE BENEFITS OF THESE FABULOUS FUNGI, TRY TO EAT ABOUT 2 OUNCES OF MUSHROOMS A DAY.

CURRY QUINOA STUFFED PEPPERS
WITH CABBAGE SLAW & SPINACH PESTO

CURRY QUINOA STUFFED PEPPERS

Serves 6

3 orange bell peppers, halved, stemmed and seeded

1½ roma tomatoes, quartered

1 Tbsp curry powder

1 large clove garlic, minced

2 tsp coconut oil

2 cups water

1 cup quinoa

3 oz raw spinach leaves, chopped

½ cup fresh green peas *or* edamame

3 Tbsp olive oil

1 Tbsp lemon juice

¾ tsp sea salt

Smoked paprika

• Preheat the oven to 400°F. On a baking sheet lined with parchment paper, place bell pepper halves and roast for 25 minutes. Remove from oven and set aside. Keep the oven on.

• While the peppers are roasting, in a food processor, combine tomatoes, curry powder, and garlic and blend until smooth.

• Transfer contents of food processor to a large pot over medium-low heat. Simmer for 5 minutes, then stir in the coconut oil.

• Add water and quinoa and bring to a boil. Reduce heat and simmer uncovered about 15 minutes, or until the water is fully absorbed into the quinoa. Remove from heat, cover, and let rest 5 minutes.

• Add spinach leaves, peas *or* edamame, olive oil, and lemon juice to the pot. Season with sea salt and toss until well combined.

• Stuff each roasted bell pepper half with a heaping ⅓ cup of quinoa mixture, garnish with a dash of smoked paprika powder on top. Return to the oven and roast for 10 more minutes.

• Remove from oven, serve on top of Cabbage Slaw, and drizzle with Spinach Pesto.

SPINACH PESTO

Makes 1½ cups

4 cups fresh spinach leaves

3 Tbsp lemon juice

⅔ cup olive oil

½ tsp sea salt

• In a high-power blender, combine all ingredients and puree, first on low then gradually raising the speed to high, until smooth and creamy.

• Use immediately or transfer to a glass jar with a tight seal and store in the refrigerator for up to 3 days.

CABBAGE SLAW WITH SCHIZANDRA FRUIT DRESSING

Serves 4-6

1 small head green or white
  cabbage, shredded

5 Tbsp olive oil

3 Tbsp apple juice

2½ Tbsp orange juice

2 Tbsp lemon juice

2 tsp ume plum vinegar

¼ tsp schizandra powder

2-3 pinches white pepper

½ cup flat-leaf parsley, chopped,
  for garnish

6 Tbsp raw pine nuts, for garnish

6 Tbsp dried cranberries sweetened
  with apple juice, for garnish

• In a large salad bowl, place the shredded cabbage, drizzle with oil until moist, add the fruit juices, followed by the vinegar, schizandra, and white pepper. Toss until well coated.

• When plating, garnish with parsley, pine nuts, and dried cranberries.

SCHIZANDRA IN PARTICULAR IS VIEWED AS QUINTESSENTIAL TO THE PRESERVATION OF JING, THE PRIMORDIAL PEP IN THE STEP, THE LIFE-FORCE ENERGY.

DAIKON NIMONO
WITH JING TIME RICE & CARROT ZIP-ZAP DRESSING

This macrobiotic meal provides satisfying mineral nutrition, robust earthy flavors, and textural balance. The Daikon Nimono takes almost 2 hours to prepare, but everything else can be made while it is simmering.

DAIKON NIMONO

Serves 4-6

1½ lb daikon root, peeled and sliced
    into thick, even rounds

6 cups Kombu Dashi (page 47)

3 Tbsp tamari

3 tsp rice vinegar

1½ tsp raw honey

3 Tbsp mirin

Carrot Zip-Zap Dressing (page 184),
    for serving

2-3 avocados, sliced, for serving

Fine & Mellow Kraut (page 79),
    for serving

1 green onion, sliced into thin rounds,
    for garnish

Black sesame seeds, for garnish

- In a large pot over high heat, combine the daikon, Kombu Dashi, tamari, rice vinegar, and honey and bring to a boil. Reduce heat and simmer for 10 minutes.
- Reduce heat to low and simmer for 1½ hours, or until the liquid is mostly gone and the daikon is golden brown. Pour the mirin over the mixture, remove from heat, and set aside.
- While daikon is simmering, prepare the Jing Time Rice and Carrot Zip-Zap Dressing.
- On each serving plate, arrange ½ avocado, sliced; 3-4 Daikon Nimono slices drizzled with braising liquid and garnished with sliced green onion; ½ cup Jing Time Rice; and a dollop of Fine & Mellow Kraut. Pour on a little Carrot Zip-Zap Dressing to grace everything and garnish with a pinch of black sesame seeds.

JING TIME RICE

Makes 3 cups, serves 6

2 cups water

½ cup black rice, rinsed and drained

3 Tbsp wild rice, rinsed and drained

3 Tbsp brown rice, rinsed and drained

2 Tbsp red rice, rinsed and drained

- In a medium pot over high heat, combine all ingredients and bring to a boil.
- Reduce heat and simmer for 25 minutes, or until the water is fully absorbed and the rice is soft.
- Remove from heat and set aside until ready to serve.

RED RICE, QUINOA & GREEN BEAN SALAD

This salad may be served warm or at room temperature as a side dish, or over a bed of mixed greens with sliced avocado.

Makes 6 cups, serves 4-6

⅔ cup quinoa

½ cup Camargue red rice

4 oz green beans

3⅓ cups water, divided

4 Tbsp olive oil

6 oz sweet onion, peeled and chopped

4 whole dried apricots, chopped

2 spring onions, thinly sliced

2 oz hazelnuts, lightly toasted, peeled, and roughly chopped

1 oz arugula

½ garlic clove, crushed

Juice of ½ orange

2 Tbsp lemon juice

2 tsp orange zest

1½ tsp sea salt

1 tsp white wine vinegar

¼ tsp white pepper

• In a small saucepan, bring 1⅓ cups water to a boil and add quinoa. Simmer uncovered for 15-20 minutes, or until the bottom of the grains begins to crackle. Remove from heat, cover, and let steam for 10 minutes, then fluff with a fork.

• In a separate small saucepan, rinse and drain Camargue red rice, add 1 cup water, and bring to a boil, then reduce heat and simmer half-covered for 20 minutes until rice is soft. Remove from heat, cover, and let steam for 10 minutes, then fluff with a fork.

• In a separate small saucepan with a steamer basket, steam green beans over 1 cup of boiling water for about 3 minutes, until tender and bright green. Remove from heat, rinse under cool water, and set aside.

• In a skillet over medium-high heat, sauté sweet onion in 2 Tbsp olive oil with 2 pinches sea salt for about 8 minutes, or until lightly golden and fragrant. Remove from heat and set aside.

• In a large mixing bowl, combine cooked grains, steamed green beans, and sautéed onion with dried apricots, spring onions, hazelnuts, and arugula. Season with remaining olive oil, garlic, citrus juices, vinegar, salt, and pepper, and toss until well combined.

MOROCCAN VEGETABLES & BAKED YAM SALAD
WITH CASHEW SUMAC YOGURT SAUCE

BAKED YAM SALAD

Serves 4-6

4-6 large handfuls
   mixed greens

2-3 yams, scrubbed and
   pierced a few times
   with a fork

2-3 Tbsp raw pistachios,
   chopped, for garnish

Lemon zest, for garnish

- Preheat the oven to 425ºF. Place the yams on a baking sheet and roast for 40-60 minutes, or until soft.
- Remove from oven and set aside to cool slightly. Slice the yams in half lengthwise.
- On individual serving plates, arrange greens, top with a roasted yam half and a scoop of Moroccan Vegetables (raw or roasted), drizzle with Cashew Sumac Yogurt Sauce, and garnish with pistachios and lemon zest.

MOROCCAN VEGETABLES

Makes 4 cups roasted or 8 cups raw, serving 4-6

2 cups zucchini, cubed

2 cups summer squash,
   diced

2 medium portobello
   mushrooms, stemmed
   and cubed

1⅓ cup red bell peppers,
   chopped

1 cup flat-leaf parsley,
   minced

1 cup shallots, thinly
   sliced

½ cup cilantro, minced

2 garlic cloves, halved
   and smashed

5 Tbsp olive oil

5 Tbsp lemon juice

1 tsp salt

1 tsp ground coriander

1 tsp ground sweet paprika

1 tsp ground cinnamon

1 tsp cumin seeds

½ tsp freshly ground
   black pepper

½ tsp ground cumin

- If roasting, preheat oven to 425ºF. In a mixing bowl, combine all ingredients and toss until well coated. Set aside to marinate for 20-30 minutes.
- Transfer marinated vegetables to a baking sheet lined with parchment paper and roast for 15 minutes, or until lightly golden brown and tender.

CAN BE SERVED RAW, AFTER MARINATING, FOR MAXIMUM ENZYMATIC BENEFITS, OR ROASTED AND SERVED HOT ON A CHILLY DAY.

CASHEW SUMAC YOGURT SAUCE

Makes about 2 cups

½ cup water

½ cup raw cashews, soaked
    4-6 hours, drained,
    and rinsed

¼ cup lemon juice

2 Tbsp raw tahini

2 Tbsp olive oil

1 tsp apple cider vinegar

1 tsp unpasteurized
    white miso

½ tsp nutritional yeast

¼ tsp salt

1 Tbsp flat-leaf parsley,
    minced (optional)

1½ tsp dill weed, minced
    (optional)

¼ tsp mustard seeds
    (optional)

¼ tsp fennel seeds
    (optional)

1 pinch ground sumac,
    for garnish

- In a high-power blender, combine water, cashews, lemon juice, tahini, oil, vinegar, miso, yeast, and salt and puree, first on low then gradually raising the speed to high, to make a smooth, yogurt-like cream.
- For adventurous palates, add the parsley, dill, and mustard and fennel seeds and blend on low for 1 minute, or until well combined.
- Serve immediately, garnished with a sprinkle of sumac, or transfer to a glass jar with a tight seal and store in the refrigerator for up to 5 days.

SESAME TOFU
WITH ASIAN STIR-FRIED VEGETABLES

SESAME TOFU

Serves 4

14 oz firm tofu, cut into ½-inch slices

3 Tbsp tamari

2 Tbsp mirin

2 Tbsp raw honey

2 Tbsp white sesame seeds

1 Tbsp fresh ginger, finely grated

2 tsp toasted sesame oil

1 Tbsp coconut oil

• In a small jar, combine tamari, mirin, honey, sesame seeds, ginger, and sesame oil and shake. In a shallow pan, lay out the tofu slices, cover with the tamari marinade, and set aside for 30 minutes, flipping the tofu halfway through.

• In a skillet over medium-high heat, warm the coconut oil. Add marinated tofu pieces and sear on all sides 5-7 minutes, or until the tofu is golden.

• Reduce the heat to low and add the marinade to the pan. Cook for 3 minutes, but take care that it does not burn, as the honey caramelizes easily. Set aside until ready to serve.

ASIAN STIR-FRIED VEGETABLES

Serves 4

2 medium bunches spinach, washed but not dried

1 bunch asparagus, cut diagonally into large chunks

1-inch piece fresh ginger, peeled and finely sliced

1 large head of broccoli, separated into small florets, stalks chopped into batons

1 bunch spring onions, cut diagonally into large chunks

¼ lb shiitake mushrooms, cut into large chunks

3 Tbsp unrefined sesame oil

2 Tbsp olive oil

1 Tbsp tamari

1 Tbsp lemon juice

1 tsp toasted sesame oil

Salt and freshly ground black pepper

Chopped toasted almonds and sesame seeds, for garnish

• Heat a large frying pan or wok over a medium-high to high flame. Add 1 Tbsp sesame oil to coat the pan, or enough to form a thin puddle in bottom of wok. Add the wet spinach in batches. Cook for 2 minutes stirring constantly, or until just wilted. Transfer the cooked spinach to a colander lined with cheesecloth or paper towels to drain.

• Gently compress the spinach in the cheesecloth or paper towels to expel the excess liquid. Transfer the drained spinach to a large mixing bowl and set aside.

• Return the frying pan or wok to the flame. When hot, add another ½ Tbsp sesame oil and the ginger and asparagus. Stir-fry for 2-3 minutes, until lightly cooked but still crunchy. Remove from heat and transfer to the bowl with the spinach. Repeat with the broccoli, spring onions, and shiitake mushrooms, adding everything to the large mixing bowl.

• Dress the vegetables with olive oil, tamari, lemon juice, sesame oil, salt, and pepper, and toss to combine.

• On individual serving plates, arrange Stir-Fried Vegetables, top with sautéed Sesame Tofu, and garnish with toasted almonds and sesame seeds.

SPICED CHICKPEAS & VEGETABLE SALAD
WITH LEMON MARINADE

Serves 4-6

¼ lb dried chickpeas, soaked overnight
  in cold water and drained

Water, as needed

1 tsp baking soda

⅔ lb radishes, cut into ½-inch dice

2 large tomatoes, cut into ½-inch dice

2 small cucumbers, cut into
  ½-inch dice

1 small red onion, peeled and cut into
  ½-inch dice

1 red pepper, deseeded and cut into
  ½-inch dice

⅓ cup cilantro, roughly chopped

¼ cup flat-leaf parsley,
  roughly chopped

⅓ cup olive oil

¼ cup lemon juice

2 Tbsp sherry vinegar

Zest of 2 lemons

1 clove garlic, crushed

¼ tsp salt, plus more to taste

Freshly ground black pepper

1½ tsp ground allspice

1 tsp ground cardamom

1 tsp ground cumin

• Place the chickpeas in a large saucepan over medium heat and cover with twice the volume of water. Stir in baking soda. Bring to a boil and simmer, periodically skimming off any foam, for 1 hour, or until tender. Remove from heat and drain.

• In a large serving bowl, add the radishes, tomatoes, cucumbers, onion, red pepper, cilantro, and parsley, and toss to combine.

• In a jar or container with a tight seal, combine 3 Tbsp olive oil, the lemon juice, vinegar, lemon zest, and garlic. Season with salt and black pepper, seal, and shake well. Pour the lemon marinade over the vegetables and toss lightly.

• In a wide, shallow bowl, combine the allspice, cardamom, cumin, and ¼ tsp salt and stir until well combined.

• In a skillet over medium heat, warm the remaining 2 Tbsp olive oil. Add the chickpeas and lightly fry for 2-3 minutes, gently shaking the pan throughout so they cook evenly and don't stick. Remove from heat.

• In batches, toss the warmed chickpeas in the spice mixture until well coated.

• Add the spiced chickpeas to the bowl with the dressed vegetables and serve.

ROASTED VEGETABLE & ARUGULA SALAD
WITH EASY-PEASY TAHINI DRESSING

Serves 6-8

4 small beets, peeled and cut into
    thin wedges

4 small fennel bulbs, cut into wedges

2 small red onions, peeled and cut
    into 8 wedges

1 small butternut squash, skin on,
    halved lengthwise, seeds discarded,
    cut into 1-inch-thick spears

1 lb cherry tomatoes

6-8 handfuls arugula

½ cup + 3 Tbsp olive oil

2 Tbsp balsamic vinegar

2 Tbsp lemon juice

Sea salt and freshly ground
    black pepper

- Preheat the oven to 400°F.
- In a large mixing bowl, combine beets, fennel, onions, and squash, drizzle with ½ cup olive oil, season generously with sea salt and freshly ground black pepper, and toss until well coated.
- In a large roasting tray lined with parchment paper, spread out the vegetables, cover tightly with foil, and roast for 40 minutes, or until veggies are tender when pierced with a knife.
- Remove the foil, scatter the cherry tomatoes over the other veggies, and roast uncovered for 15-20 more minutes, or until everything is a little caramelized. Remove from oven and set aside to cool slightly.
- In a large mixing bowl, toss warm veggies with 2 Tbsp balsamic vinegar until well combined.
- In a separate mixing bowl, toss arugula with 3 Tbsp olive oil and 2 Tbsp lemon juice. Season with sea salt and freshly ground black pepper to taste.
- Serve scoops of roasted vegetables atop beds of dressed arugula, and drizzle with Easy-Peasy Tahini Dressing.

EASY-PEASY TAHINI DRESSING

Makes 1¼ cups

½ cup water

⅓ cup raw tahini

2 Tbsp lemon juice

½ clove garlic, minced

¼ tsp sea salt

¼ tsp freshly ground black pepper

- In a high-power blender, combine all ingredients and blend until mixture is smooth, with a runny consistency.
- Use immediately or transfer to a glass jar with a tight seal and store in the refrigerator for up to 5 days.

SPIRALIZED SQUASH NOODLES
WITH SAUTÉED LEEKS, FEISTY BREADCRUMBS & PORCINI CREAM SAUCE

This satisfying vegetable noodle dish is low in carbohydrates and packed full of enzymatic activity, thanks to the living zucchini spirals. The Porcini Cream Sauce adds full-flavored body; the Feisty Breadcrumbs create texture; and the Sautéed Leeks sing, creating an opera of textural mouth feel, warm comfort, and enveloping flavors.

SPIRALIZED SQUASH NOODLES

Serves 4-6

4 large zucchini, trimmed, peeled, and halved crosswise, at room temperature

- Preheat the oven to 150°F. Using a spiralizer or similar tool, transform the zucchini into spiral noodles. Place noodles in an oven-safe bowl and set aside.
- About 20 minutes before serving, place the bowl of spiral noodles in the oven to warm.

SAUTÉED LEEKS

3 leeks, washed, trimmed, and cut into ½-inch medallions, including green parts

3 Tbsp olive oil

4-5 pinches sea salt

2-3 pinches freshly ground black pepper

Chopped parsley (optional), for garnish

- In a large skillet over medium heat, warm the oil. Add leek medallions, placing them flat, and sauté for about 6-7 minutes or until edges are slightly browned. Flip the medallions, season with salt and black pepper, and brown on the other side, gently shaking the pan throughout, until the leeks remain bright green and fresh with slightly browned edges. Remove from heat.
- On each serving plate, pour a little Porcini Cream Sauce, top with 1 cup Spiralized Squash Noodles, ⅓ cup Feisty Breadcrumbs (page 66), and ¾ cup Sautéed Leeks, and garnish with chopped parsley, if desired.

PORCINI CREAM SAUCE

1 cup hot water

1 oz dried porcini mushrooms

⅔ cup raw cashews, soaked 4-6 hours, drained, and rinsed

½ cup nut mylk (pages 174, 177)

4 Tbsp olive oil

2 cloves garlic, minced

1 tsp salt

¼ tsp white pepper

- In a small mixing bowl, add the hot water to the porcini mushrooms and set aside to steep for 30 minutes.
- In a high-power blender, combine the mushrooms and steeping liquid with remianing ingredients and puree, first on low then gradually raising the speed to high, until smooth.
- Transfer to a pot with a lid and cover to keep warm until ready to serve.
- Leftover sauce can be stored in a tightly sealed container in the refrigerator for up to 4 days.

HEIRLOOM BEANS
WITH WILTED CHARD

Serves 4-6

4 cups water

1 cup dried beans, any kind, soaked
    overnight, drained, and rinsed

3 cloves garlic, smashed

2 bay leaves

½ tsp black peppercorns

1 tsp sea salt

¼ cup olive oil

¼ yellow onion, thinly sliced
    lengthwise

1 tsp sherry vinegar

¼ tsp rubbed sage*

5 leaves and stems Swiss chard,
    chopped into large pieces

¼ cup flat-leaf parsley, minced

1 Tbsp lemon juice

½ tsp freshly ground black pepper

1 large head romaine lettuce

½ cup Sea Czar Dressing (page 75)

2-4 heirloom tomatoes, sliced

* If using ground dried sage, use
about half the quantity specified.

• In a medium pot over medium heat, combine water, beans, garlic, bay leaves, peppercorns, and ½ tsp salt. Bring to a boil and cook at a steady boil for 10 minutes.

• Reduce heat and simmer for 25-30 more minutes, or until beans are very soft. Remove from heat, discard bay leaves and peppercorns, and set aside to cool.

• In a medium skillet over medium heat, warm 1 Tbsp olive oil. Add onion, sherry vinegar, sage, and a few pinches of salt and sauté for 5 minutes, or until nicely golden brown. Add Swiss chard, toss until well combined, and remove from heat immediately, as the chard cooks very quickly.

• Drain the cooled beans and transfer to the skillet with the chard mixture. Season with the remaining oil, parsley, lemon juice, salt, and black pepper, and gently fold to combine.

• Divide lettuce among serving plates, drizzle with Sea Czar Dressing, add a layer of sliced tomatoes, and top with 1 cup of chard and bean mixture, creating a spontaneous heap of scrumptiousness.

THIS DISH CAN BE MADE WITH ANY KIND OF BEANS IN THE PANTRY, FROM PLAIN WHITE OR BLACK BEANS TO HEIRLOOM VARIETALS WITH GREAT NAMES LIKE ORCA BEANS, CRANBERRY BEANS, SCARLET RUNNER BEANS, AND EVEN TONGUES OF FIRE BEANS! SO WHY NOT EXPLORE ALL THE BEAUTIFUL BEAN VARIETIES THE WORLD HAS TO OFFER?

AFROFUSION RICE BOWL

The flavors of sub-Saharan Africa come together in this inspired rice bowl—a light, healthy sampler of traditional fare. Much of this satisfying meal can be made ahead, or a simplified version consisting of just the Yellow Rice, Komastuna, and Peanut Sauce can be prepared when time is more limited. To serve: In bowls, arrange ½ cup South African Yellow Rice, ¼ cup Roasted Harvest Vegetables, 1 cup East African Kachumbari, and ½ cup West African Komastuna Mustard Greens. Drizzle with West African Peanut Sauce and garnish, if desired, with sliced raw okra and a pinch of black cumin seeds.

SOUTH AFRICAN YELLOW RICE

Makes 3 cups, serves 4-6

2 tsp red palm fruit oil

¼ yellow onion, diced

1 Tbsp coconut nectar
   or coconut sugar

1 tsp fresh ginger, finely
   grated

½ tsp turmeric powder

¼ tsp cumin seeds

1 dash white pepper

1 pinch smoked salt

½ tsp salt

2½ cups hot water,
   vegetable stock, or
   Simplicity Broth
   (page 57)

1 cup brown basmati rice

• In a large skillet over medium heat, warm the oil. Add the onion, coconut nectar, ginger, turmeric, cumin seeds, white pepper, smoked salt, and ½ tsp salt. Sauté for 5 minutes, or until lightly golden and fragrant.

• Add the rice to the skillet and toss to combine. Toast for 3 more minutes.

• Add the hot water or stock to the skillet and bring to a boil. Reduce heat and simmer for about 25 minutes, or until the rice is tender and fluffy. Remove from heat and set aside until ready to serve.

ROASTED HARVEST VEGETABLES

Makes 4 cups, serves 4-6

3 cups butternut squash,
   peeled and cubed

2 cups yam, peeled and
   cubed

6 oz shallots, peeled and
   chopped

2 cloves garlic, minced

4 Tbsp coconut oil

1 tsp salt

½ tsp freshly ground
   black pepper

½ tsp smoked paprika

2-4 dashes chipotle powder

• Preheat the oven to 400°F. In a mixing bowl, combine all ingredients and toss until well coated.

• Transfer to a baking sheet lined with parchment paper and roast for 25 minutes. Remove from oven and set aside until ready to serve.

KOMASTUNA IS A JAPANESE VERSION OF MUSTARD GREENS, SPICY YET MILD IN FLAVOR, AND NEARLY IDENTICAL TO SPINACH IN APPEARANCE AND TEXTURE. FOR DISHES TRADITIONALLY MADE WITH SPINACH, SUBSTITUTING KOMASTUNA INSTEAD ADDS A NICE MINERAL BOOST.

WEST AFRICAN KOMASTUNA MUSTARD GREENS

Serves 4-6

1 Tbsp red palm fruit oil

1 yellow onion, chopped

1 tsp fresh ginger,
    finely grated

½ tsp sea salt

¼ tsp freshly ground
    black pepper

½ green bell pepper, seeded
    and diced

1 bunch komastuna
    (or spinach), chopped

2 roma tomatoes, chopped

- In a large skillet with a lid over medium-low heat, warm the oil. Add the onion and ginger and season with salt and black pepper. Sauté for 10 minutes, or until lightly golden and fragrant.
- Add bell pepper and sauté for 3-5 more minutes.
- Stir in the komastuna and tomatoes, and adjust salt and black pepper to taste.
- Remove from heat, cover, and set aside for a few minutes, until the komastuna becomes warm and wilted.

EAST AFRICAN KACHUMBARI

Serves 4-6

½ small head cabbage,
    shredded

2 roma tomatoes, sliced into
    thin wedges

1 Persian cucumber, diced

½ medium sweet onion,
    chopped

½ green bell pepper, diced

⅓ cup cilantro, chopped

3 Tbsp lime juice

1 Tbsp jalapeño pepper,
    seeded and minced

1 tsp sherry vinegar

¾ tsp sea salt

- In a large serving bowl, combine all ingredients and toss until well blended.

WEST AFRICAN PEANUT SAUCE

Serves 4-6

⅔ cup water

½ cup natural peanut butter

½ roma tomato

2 tsp red palm fruit oil

½ tsp salt

10 dashes ground cayenne

- In a high-power blender, combine all ingredients and puree, first on low and then gradually raising the speed to high, until smooth.

UNREFINED RED PALM FRUIT OIL IS RICH IN OLEIC AND PALMITIC ACIDS, WITH LESS SATURATED FAT THAN REFINED PALM KERNEL OIL, AND IF PRODUCED WITH FAIR-TRADE, SUSTAINABLY HARVESTED METHODS, IT POSES NO THREAT TO ORANGUTANS OR FORESTS. WITH LEVELS OF CAROTENE AND LYCOPENE SURPASSING THOSE FOUND IN CARROTS AND TOMATOES, IT IS ALSO LOADED WITH TOCOTRIENOLS, A BIOAVAILABLE FORM OF VITAMIN E. STUDIES SHOW THAT IT CAN HELP PREVENT CLOGGED ARTERIES AND PROTECT THE BRAIN'S NERVE CELLS. THESE HEALTH BENEFITS ARE LOST IN THE REFINEMENT THAT PRODUCES THE PALM KERNEL OIL COMMONLY FOUND IN PROCESSED FOODS.

TRUFFLE HUNTER'S WILD RICE

Makes 3½ cups, serves 2-4

2 quarts water

1½ cups wild rice, thoroughly rinsed and drained

1½ cups avocado, cubed

2 Tbsp flat-leaf parsley, minced

3 tsp ume plum vinegar

2 tsp flaxseed oil

½ tsp truffle oil

4 pinches smoked sea salt

- In a large pot over high heat, combine water and rice and bring to a boil.
- Reduce heat and simmer half covered for 45 minutes to 1 hour, or until all the rice kernels have split open. Remove from heat, cover, and let steam for 10 minutes. Drain any excess moisture.
- In a large bowl, gently mix the cooked rice with the remaining ingredients and until well combined.
- Mold the warm rice mixture into 4-6 serving portions as desired. Serve warm, with Woodsmoke Shiitake Mushrooms (page 103) or paired with West African Komastuna Mustard Greens (page 121) and Moroccan Vegetables (page 110).

HAZELNUT SAGE BEET SALAD

Serves 4-6

4 large red beets

½ cup raw hazelnuts

1 cup fennel, shaved

½ medium red onion, shaved

4 Tbsp olive oil

4 Tbsp lemon juice

2 Tbsp flaxseed oil

2 Tbsp rice vinegar

1 Tbsp fresh sage leaves, chiffonaded

2 tsp fresh garlic chives, minced

1 tsp salt

½ tsp white pepper

- In a medium pot over high heat, cover beets with water and bring to a boil, then reduce heat and simmer until tender, about 45 minutes to 1 hour, or until a fork slides in easily. Remove from heat, drain, and set aside until cool enough to handle.
- Rinse beets under cool water and peel off and discard skins. Cut beets into chunks and place in a large serving bowl.
- In a dry skillet over low heat, toast hazelnuts for about 10 minutes, or until fragrant, stirring constantly so they don't burn. Remove from heat. Using a kitchen towel, rub hazelnuts until the papery skins fall off. Add hazelnuts to the serving bowl.
- Add remaining ingredients to the bowl and toss gently to combine. Serve warm.

SEASONAL HARVEST BOWL
WITH ONE-TWO PUNCH BALSAMIC DRESSING

This satisfying meal embraces the autumn harvest with fresh dark leafy greens, hearty grains, and roasted fall veggies. Delivered with classic One-Two Punch Balsamic Dressing and topped with crunchy seeds and chewy cranberries, a dark daylight-saving night just got a little brighter.

Serves 4-6

½ medium head cauliflower, chopped

½ medium head broccoli, chopped

1 large sweet potato, peeled and
   chopped

2 Tbsp coconut oil

Sea salt and freshly ground
   black pepper to taste

¾ cup quinoa

¾ cup organic black rice

3¼ cups water, divided

3 handfuls each kale and arugula,
   for serving

6 Tbsp dried cranberries, for garnish

6 Tbsp toasted pumpkin seeds,
   for garnish

6 Tbsp raw sunflower seeds,
   for garnish

Spike Gourmet Natural Seasoning,
   to taste (optional)

• Preheat the oven to 400°F. In a large mixing bowl, combine cauliflower, broccoli, and sweet potato with coconut oil, salt, and pepper, and toss until well coated. Transfer to a baking tray lined with parchment paper and roast for 40 minutes, or until tender and golden brown. Remove from oven and set aside to keep warm until ready to serve.

• While the veggies are roasting, cook the grains: In a medium saucepan, bring 1½ cups of water to a boil and add the quinoa. Reduce heat and simmer uncovered for 15-20 minutes, or until the water is absorbed and the bottom begins to crackle. Remove from heat, cover, and let steam for 10 minutes.

• At the same time, in a separate saucepan, rinse and drain the black rice twice, then add 1¾ cups water and bring to a boil. Reduce heat, and simmer half-covered for 25 minutes or until the water is absorbed and the bottom of the grains begins to crackle. Remove heat, cover, and let steam for 10 minutes.

• In a large mixing bowl, combine black rice and quinoa, cover, and set aside to keep warm until ready to serve.

• In serving bowls, arrange the kale and arugula, top with scoops of cooked grains and roasted vegetables, garnish with cranberries, pumpkin and sunflower seeds, and drizzle with One-Two Punch Balsamic Dressing. For added Ashram flavor, add a final dash of Spike Gourmet Natural Seasoning!

ONE-TWO PUNCH BALSAMIC DRESSING

Makes ¾ cup

½ cup olive oil

¼ cup balsamic vinegar

• With a simple one-two punch, combine olive oil and balsamic vinegar in a glass jar with a tight seal and shake well.

6

SWEETS & SNACKS

24-CARROT BIRTHDAY CAKE
WITH LEMON ZING FROSTING

Makes one 6-inch-diameter mini cake, serves 4-8

8 medium carrots, peeled and cut into chunks

2 green apples, cored and cut into chunks

¼ cup raw walnuts, finely chopped

¼ cup dried shredded coconut

2 Tbsp raw walnuts, crushed

2 Tbsp water

2 Tbsp Lemon Zing Frosting

1-2 Tbsp coconut sugar

1 Tbsp dried pineapple, chopped

1½ tsp ground cinnamon

1-2 tsp raw honey, to taste

½ tsp fresh ginger, finely grated

½ tsp orange zest

¼ tsp lemon zest

¼ tsp vanilla extract

¼ tsp salt

3 pinches freshly grated nutmeg

2 dashes ground clove

THESE DESSERTS ARE GENERALLY ON THE LESS-SWEET SIDE, SO FEEL FREE TO ADD A BIT MORE HONEY.

THIS CAKE HAS A NICE TONIFYING LEMON KICK TO BOOST LIVER FUNCTION.

FOR A FULL-SIZE CAKE, DOUBLE THE CAKE RECIPE AND USE TWO 9-INCH-DIAMETER SPRINGFORM PANS. WHEN MAKING A FULL-SIZE CAKE, IT'S HELPFUL TO PLACE THE TOP LAYER BY FIRST CUTTING IT INTO PIECES AND REASSEMBLING THEM ON TOP OF THE BOTTOM LAYER. ONCE IN PLACE, USE A SPATULA TO SMOOTH IT ALL TOGETHER, THEN COVER IT WITH FROSTING, WHICH FIXES EVERYTHING!

• Make the Lemon Zing Frosting first, because some is used in the cake batter.

• With a juicer, juice the carrots and apples. Pour juice into a 1-quart jar and reserve for making Carrot Apple Lime Cooler (page 160).

• Remove the carrot and apple pulp from the juicer (including the pulp inside the machine); in total, 1½ cups of pulp is needed.

• In a medium mixing bowl, combine the carrot and apple pulp with the remaining batter ingredients and mix until well combined.

• Line the bottom of 2 small (6-inch) springform pans with parchment paper. Divide cake batter equally between the pans, and press the batter into each pan, smoothing the batter evenly across the top.

• Transfer 1 of the cake layers to a plate and peel off the paper. Spread a thin layer of Lemon Zing Frosting on top before gently placing the second cake layer. Frost the whole cake with the remaining frosting, sculpting it evenly all around.

• Before serving, decorate as desired with chopped walnuts or pecans, shredded coconut, ground cinnamon, lemon zest, and/or carrot ribbons.

LEMON ZING FROSTING

Makes about 1½ cups, enough to frost 2 mini cakes
or 1 full-size cake

½ cup blanched almonds, soaked 8 hours, drained, and rinsed

½ cup raw cashews, soaked 4-6 hours, drained, and rinsed

⅓ cup water

¼ cup lemon juice

3-4 Tbsp raw honey, maple syrup, or coconut nectar

1 Tbsp raw pine nuts, soaked 4 hours, drained, and rinsed

2 oz fresh young coconut meat (*or* frozen coconut smoothie packs)

1 tsp vanilla extract

¼ tsp ground vanilla beans

3-4 drops liquid stevia

1-2 drops lemon oil

- In a high-power blender, combine all ingredients and puree, first on low then gradually raising the speed to high, until smooth and creamy.
- Use immediately or transfer to a container with a tight seal and store in the refrigerator for up to 3-5 days.
- Leftover frosting can also be used as a topping for the Strawberry Chocolate Tart (page 141).

BLUE MERMAID PARFAIT
WITH SCHIZANDRA BERRY SAUCE

Serves 2

Blue Mermaid Cream

Schizandra Berry Sauce

1 cup fresh blackberries

1 kiwi, peeled and sliced

Lime zest, for garnish

- In a parfait glass, layer dollops of Blue Mermaid Cream and drizzles of Schizandra Berry Sauce with blackberries and kiwi slices.
- Drizzle with Schizandra Berry Sauce, garnish with lime zest, and serve.

BLUE MERMAID CREAM

Makes 1 cup

4 oz young coconut, fresh or frozen
  (*or* frozen coconut smoothie packs)

½ cup nut mylk (pages 174, 177)

1 tsp raw honey

½ tsp vanilla extract

2 pinches ground vanilla beans

1-2 capsules Blue Majik* (an extract
  of spirulina)

- In a blender, combine all ingredients and blend until smooth and creamy.
- Use immediately or transfer to a glass jar with a tight seal and store in the refrigerator for up to 3 days.

* Adding more Blue Majik will produce a brighter blue, but the algae flavor will be slightly more pronounced.

BLUE MAJIK IS DERIVED FROM SPIRULINA, WITH A CONCENTRATION OF PHYCOCYANIN—THE NATURAL BLUE PIGMENT FOUND IN BLUE-GREEN ALGAES—AN ANTIOXIDANT PIGMENT WITH ANTI-INFLAMMATORY PROPERTIES THAT ARE BENEFICIAL TO ANYONE SUFFERING FROM CONDITIONS SUCH AS FIBROMYALGIA, ARTHRITIC JOINTS, MUSCLE OR BACK PAIN, ALLERGIES, AND EVEN FREQUENT MIGRAINES. IT IS ALSO EXCELLENT AS A POST-WORKOUT SUPPLEMENT TO REDUCE MUSCLE SORENESS.

SCHIZANDRA BERRY SAUCE

Serves 2

4 oz frozen raspberries,
  slightly thawed

¼ tsp schizandra powder

2 Tbsp raw honey

1 Tbsp water

1 Tbsp lime juice

2 tsp chia seeds

- In a blender, combine all ingredients except the chia seeds, and blend until well mixed.
- Transfer contents to a glass jar. Fold the chia seeds into the mixture, seal, and allow to set in the refrigerator for at least 2 hours before serving.
- Can be stored in the refrigerator for up to 3 days.

LEMON CHEEZECAKE STRAWBERRY BITES

Makes about 2 cups

2 oz fresh young coconut meat
   (*or* frozen coconut smoothie packs)

½ cup blanched almonds, soaked
   8 hours, drained, and rinsed

½ cup raw cashews, soaked 4-6 hours,
   drained, and rinsed

1 Tbsp raw pine nuts, soaked 4 hours,
   drained, and rinsed

⅓ cup lemon juice

¼ cup water

2-3 Tbsp raw honey, to taste

¼ tsp ground vanilla beans

2-3 drops lemon oil

1 quart fresh strawberries, halved

1 cup raw pecan halves, for garnish

2-3 Tbsp bee pollen (optional,
   if available), for garnish

• In a high-power blender, combine the coconut, almonds, cashews, lemon juice, water, honey, pine nuts, ground vanilla beans, and lemon oil, and puree, first on low then gradually raising the speed to high, until smooth and creamy.

• Transfer to a pastry bag or a plastic freezer bag and snip off a corner.

• Pipe a dollop of lemon cheezecake onto each strawberry half, and garnish with a pecan half and a sprinkle of bee pollen.

• Leftover cheezecake can be stored in a tightly sealed container in the refrigerator for up to 5 days.

BEES COLLECT POLLEN FROM FLOWER ANTHERS, STORING IT ON THEIR HIND LEGS. UPON RETURN TO THE HIVE IT IS SORTED, MIXED WITH NECTAR AND BEE SALIVA, STORED IN HONEYCOMB CELLS, SEALED WITH A LAYER OF HONEY AND WAX, AND LEFT TO FERMENT, PRESERVED BY THE LACTIC ACID BACTERIA PRESENT IN THE BEES' SALIVARY SECRETIONS. THE END PRODUCT, CALLED "BEE BREAD," BECOMES A RICH FOOD SOURCE FOR THE HIVE. LOADED WITH VITAMINS, MINERALS, OVER 20 PERCENT PROTEIN, AMINO ACIDS, PROBIOTICS, AND AN ARRAY OF ANTIOXIDANT FLAVONOID AND PHENOLIC COMPOUNDS, BEE POLLEN IS A WELLSPRING OF NUTRITION. IT HAS LONG BEEN CONSIDERED ONE OF THE WORLD'S PREMIER LONGEVITY AND ADAPTOGENIC SUPERFOODS, WITH A WELL-RESEARCHED HISTORY. BENEFICIAL FOR ASTHMA AND SEASONAL ALLERGIES, PROPER IMMUNE FUNCTION, PREVENTING HEART DISEASE, ENHANCING ATHLETIC PERFORMANCE, RELIEVING SIDE EFFECTS OF CHEMOTHERAPY, IMPROVING MUSCLE PROTEIN AND ENERGY METABOLISM IN THE ELDERLY, IT HAS ALSO PROVED CYTOTOXIC TO TUMOR CELLS. THE GERMAN FEDERAL BOARD OF HEALTH HAS RECOGNIZED IT AS A MEDICINE. BUT BECAUSE IT IS A BEE PRODUCT, THOSE WITH BEE ALLERGIES SHOULD CAUTIOUSLY TRY ONLY A FEW GRAINS AT FIRST, IN CASE OF ADVERSE REACTION.

CHOCOLATE LIFT-OFF

Makes an excellent dip for raw walnuts, celery sticks, or green apple slices. Perfect neurotrophic afternoon pick-me-up!

Makes about ½ cup

¼ cup water

½ cup raw cacao powder

3 Tbsp almond butter

2 Tbsp raw honey

1 Tbsp Billy's Infinity Greens powder

1 Tbsp flaxseed oil

1 Tbsp goji berries

1½ tsp ground cinnamon

1 tsp maca root powder

1 tsp Om Cordyceps mushroom powder

1 tsp Om Lion's Mane mushroom powder

¼ tsp ground vanilla beans

¼ tsp bee pollen

3 dashes chipotle powder

• In a medium mixing bowl, combine all ingredients and stir until smooth.

• Set aside at room temperature for 1 hour; the mixture will set into a thick paste that can be spread in a layer on a plate or pan, chilled, and sliced like fudge.

• Serve at room temperature as a dip for walnuts, sliced green apple, or celery sticks—or simply eat by itself like a chocolate pudding for dessert.

THIS SPICED CHOCOLATE CONCOCTION IS AN ANTIOXIDANT, NEUROTROPHIC BRAIN BOOSTER THAT DELIVERS A PALPABLE FEEL-GOOD MENTAL STIMULUS WITHOUT THE JITTERY CRASH OF COFFEE. IT ALSO PROVIDES SOLID IMMUNE SYSTEM AND LONGEVITY SUPPORT, COUNTERBALANCING AND MITIGATING THE PHYSICAL DEPLETION THAT OFTEN ACCOMPANIES PERIODS OF STRESS AND OVEREXHAUSTION. THE MEDICINAL MUSHROOM KNOWN AS LION'S MANE HAS BEEN SHOWN TO INDUCE NERVE GROWTH FACTOR (NGF) SYNTHESIS IN NERVE CELLS, SUPPORTING MEMORY AND THE NERVOUS SYSTEM.

ADAPTOGENS ARE SUBSTANCES THAT ENABLE THE BODY TO ADAPT TO PHYSICAL, MENTAL, OR EMOTIONAL STRESS, RESTORING ENERGY RESERVES AT THE MITOCHONDRIAL LEVEL. WITH THE PRESSURES OF MODERN LIFE, ADAPTOGENIC HERBS, ROOTS, BERRIES, AND MUSHROOMS CAN OFFER MEANS TO STAY BALANCED AND HEALTHY. GINSENG, ELEUTHERO, SCHIZANDRA, MACA, RHODIOLA, PINE POLLEN, ASHWAGANDA, ASTRAGALUS, GYNOSTEMMA, CORDYCEPS, CHAGA, REISHI, LION'S MANE, MILK THISTLE, TULSI (HOLY BASIL), ALOE VERA, GOTU KOLA, MORINGA, BACOPA, SHATAVARI, AMLA, DONG QUAI, AND LICORICE ROOT ALL HAVE EXHIBITED POWERFUL ADAPTOGENIC PROPERTIES.

DANDY MOCHA ALMOND GELATO
WITH CHOCOLATE SYRUP

Makes 2⅓ cups, serves 4-6

1⅓ cups nut mylk (pages 174, 177)

¼ cup raw pine nuts

¼ cup raw cashews

2 Tbsp coconut oil

1 Tbsp raw honey

1 Tbsp Om Lion's Mane
   mushroom powder

4 tsp Dandy Blend Instant
   Herbal Beverage

½ oz cacao butter

¼ tsp vanilla extract

½ tsp chocolate extract

½ tsp raw cacao powder

2 pinches ground vanilla beans

10 drops liquid stevia

½ cup sliced raw almonds, for garnish

- In a high-power blender, combine ½ cup of nut mylk and all the other ingredients except the sliced almonds, and blend into a fine cream.
- Dilute the cream with another ½ cup nut mylk and blend again until well mixed. Pour the mixture into standard ice cube trays, and freeze until solid.
- In a high-power blender, break the frozen cubes and add the last ⅓ cup nut mylk. Using the blender's tamping tool to push the frozen cubes into the blades, blend the mixture until frosty and smooth, resembling gelato.
- Scoop into serving bowls, sprinkle with sliced almonds, and drizzle with Chocolate Syrup.

CHOCOLATE SYRUP

Makes ⅓ cup

2 Tbsp coconut nectar

2 Tbsp raw cacao powder

1 Tbsp flaxseed oil

1 Tbsp water

¼ tsp vanilla extract

¼ tsp chocolate extract

1 pinch sea salt

2 drops tangerine oil

- Combine all ingredients in a glass jar with a tight seal and shake to combine.
- Use immediately or store in the refrigerator for up to 2 weeks.

HONEY CURRY SNACKIE THANGS

Makes 75-90 bite-size pieces

3 sheets nori, toasted
or untoasted
½ cup Sprouted Nut
Mylk pulp* (left over
from the nut mylk—
making process;
pages 174, 177)
2 Tbsp sweet onion,
minced

1 Tbsp water
1½ tsp olive oil
½-1 tsp raw honey
½ tsp black cumin seeds
½ tsp curry powder
¼-½ tsp sea salt
1 pinch garam masala
1 pinch red pepper
flakes

* IF NO NUT MYLK PULP IS AVAILABLE,
THESE RECIPES CAN BE MADE WITH ½ CUP
GROUND SPROUTED NUTS OR SEEDS INSTEAD;
JUST OMIT THE OLIVE OIL.

• Trim the nori sheets into strips, then cut strips into squares. (Each sheet of nori should yield 25-30 squares.)
• In a small mixing bowl, combine the remaining ingredients and mash into a rustic pâté.
• Using a fork, press a little morsel of the pâté into the center of 1 nori square (shiny side up), leaving little fork ridges for texture. Place the nori square on a screened dehydrator tray. Squares can be laid quite close together, even overlapped slightly. Repeat with remaining nori squares until all ingredients have been used, filling the whole dehydrator tray.
• Dehydrate at 145ºF for 2 hours to inhibit the growth of pathogens and rapidly reduce the moisture, then reduce temperature to 115ºF and dehydrate for 12 more hours, or until crispy.
• Store up to 5-7 days in 1-2 glass jars with tight seals, and include a desiccant packet in each.

GOJI BASIL SNACKIE THANGS

Makes 75-90 bite-size pieces

3 sheets nori, toasted
or untoasted
½ cup warm water
4 sundried tomatoes
1 Tbsp goji berries
½ cup nut mylk pulp*
(left over from
the nut mylk—
making process;
pages 174, 177)
⅓ oz fresh basil leaves
1 Tbsp chopped onion

1 small clove garlic,
smashed
1 Tbsp water,
room temperature
½ Tbsp lemon juice
1½ tsp olive oil
1 tsp nutritional yeast
½ tsp oregano
½ tsp salt
¼ tsp freshly ground
black pepper

• In a small mixing bowl, combine ½ cup water, sundried tomatoes, and goji berries and set aside for 30 minutes to reconstitute. Drain.
• Trim the nori sheets into strips, then cut strips into squares. (Each sheet of nori should yield 25-30 squares.)
• In a food processor, combine the drained sundried tomatoes and goji berries with all the remaining ingredients and pulse into a slightly chunky, rustic pâté.
• Follow remaining directions above for assembling and dehydrating the nori squares, and storing the snacks.

HONEY VANILLA DARK RAW CHOCOLATE TRUFFLES

This recipe calls for special tools: an instant-read digital thermometer; chocolate molds; and a bain marie or double boiler. For the Dark Raw Chocolate, you can simply heat the raw cacao butter until it melts, stir in the other ingredients, and pour the melted chocolate into molds with the Honey Vanilla Centers—essentially skipping the tempering process—and you will still have very yummy chocolates. But if you want the chocolate to have a glossy finish and a "snap" when you bite it, pay close attention to the sequence of temperatures you must go through to achieve it. It's not really that difficult, and it's actually a fun scientific adventure!

Makes about 45 truffles

HONEY VANILLA CENTERS

⅓ cup raw cashews

¼ cup raw macadamia nuts

3 Tbsp dried shredded coconut

2½ tsp chia seeds

1 tsp tocotrienol flakes (vitamin E
    dietary supplement)

¾ tsp vanilla extract

½ tsp pine pollen

2-3 pinches ground vanilla beans

2-3 pinches sea salt

1-2 Tbsp raw honey, to taste

BEFORE BEGINNING, KEEP FIRMLY IN MIND THAT EVEN ONE DROP OF WATER IN THE CHOCOLATE WILL RUIN THE WHOLE BATCH, TURNING IT INTO SOMETHING RESEMBLING COFFEE GROUNDS. TAKE CARE THAT ALL TOOLS ARE PERFECTLY DRY WHEN WORKING WITH CHOCOLATE.

• Make the Honey Vanilla Centers: In a food processor, combine all ingredients except the honey and grind into a fine meal (the nuts will begin to release their oils). Add the honey and pulse again until the mixture forms into a soft dough. Roll into ½-inch-diameter balls. Set aside.

• Make the Dark Raw Chocolate: In a bain marie, a double boiler, or a metal mixing bowl placed atop a pot over very low heat containing about 1 inch of hot, steamy water (do not let it simmer), melt the cacao butter. When fully melted, stir in the cacao powder and the remaining ingredients.

• Temper the chocolate: Using a whisk, thoroughly combine the ingredients until everything is smooth and melted. Using an instant-read thermometer, confirm that the temperature of the chocolate comes just to 118°F.

• At this point, "seed" the chocolate by stirring in a few small pieces of a favorite well-tempered dark chocolate. Only a small amount is needed to coax the chocolate molecules to temper like the seedlings. Once the seedlings are fully assimilated, remove from heat.

• Set the bowl with the chocolate mixture on the counter to cool and continue to gently stir the chocolate while it cools to 90°F. At that point, it is ready for dipping or pouring into molds. (To speed the cooling process, the warm chocolate

DARK RAW CHOCOLATE

6 oz raw cacao butter, chopped into
  small pieces

4 oz raw cacao powder

2¼ oz coconut nectar

1½-2 oz coconut sugar, to taste

½ tsp vanilla extract

½ tsp chocolate extract

¼ tsp ground vanilla beans

¼ tsp salt

10 drops liquid stevia, or to taste

6 drops tangerine oil

½ tsp Om Lion's Mane mushroom
  powder (optional, if available)

1 capsule ashwaganda root (optional,
  if available)

bowl can be set in a larger bowl of cool water, but this will lower the temperature rapidly, so take care not to miss the magic 90°F mark!)

• Make the truffles: If using truffle molds, first fill them halfway with melted chocolate, drop in the Honey Vanilla Centers, then pour more chocolate to cover. The Honey Vanilla Centers can also be dipped into the chocolate using a toothpick and placed on baking sheets lined with wax paper; or simply place the Honey Vanilla Centers evenly spaced on baking sheets lined with wax paper and pour the chocolate over them. Whatever the method, leftover melted chocolate can be poured into bar molds (or even little Tupperware containers) and then sprinkled with dried nuts and berries.

• Immediately transfer the finished molded, dipped, or poured truffles to the refrigerator to cool and solidify, about 30-40 minutes. Do not let them cool on the counter, or the chocolate will get soft.

• When solid, pop the truffles out of the molds and wrap in foil. Store in sealed glass jars in the refrigerator for up to 90 days.

STRAWBERRY CHOCOLATE TART

Serves 8

BOTTOM CRUST

1⅓ cups fine almond flour

½ cup + 2 Tbsp raw walnuts,
    soaked 8 hours, drained, rinsed,
    and dehydrated 8-10 hours

⅓ cup + 1 Tbsp coconut sugar

3½ tsp coconut oil

3½ tsp water

1¼ tsp ground vanilla beans

¼ tsp (heaping) sea salt

GANACHE FILLING

5 oz avocado, perfectly ripe with
    no brown spots, room temperature

½ cup raw cacao powder

3 oz raw cacao butter,
    room temperature

5-6 Tbsp coconut nectar,
    room temperature, to taste

½ tsp vanilla extract

¼ tsp ground vanilla beans

2 pinches salt

4-6 drops liquid stevia, or to taste

FOR SERVING & GARNISH

2-3 cups fresh strawberries, sliced

1 cup Sprouted Vanilla Almond Mylk
    (optional, page 177), frothed

Lemon Zing Frosting (optional,
    page 127)

1 pinch bee pollen (optional)

"DESSERT FIRST" HAS LONG BEEN AN AXIOM OF THE DETOX FOOD MOVEMENT, WITH THE IDEA BEING THAT IF ONE IS GOING TO EAT DESSERT, IT SHOULD BE EATEN EITHER BY ITSELF OR LIKE AN APPETIZER BEFORE THE MAIN MEAL. TAKING THIS SENTIMENT EVEN FURTHER, WITH A RECIPE THIS WHOLESOME AND DELICIOUS, WHY NOT SIMPLY HAVE DESSERT AS THE FIRST MEAL OF THE DAY? JUST ADD SOME NUT MYLK AND CALL IT BREAKFAST.

• In a food processor, combine all ingredients and pulse into a fine meal that clumps and sticks to the sides of the bowl when the nuts have released their oils. Test to see if it holds its shape when pinched between the fingers.

• Line the bottom of a 10-inch tart pan with a removable bottom with parchment paper cut to size.

• Press the crust mixture into the pan, forming the sides first and then the bottom. Cover and set aside.

• In a clean food processor, first blend the cacao butter until it looks uniform and begins to form a thick paste.

• Add cacao powder and coconut nectar, and puree together until it rolls into a ball. Add the avocado and all remaining ingredients except strawberries and puree again, periodically scraping down the sides, until the mixture becomes a thick, smooth, buttery ganache.

• Using a rubber spatula, scoop the ganache into the crust and gently spread it evenly.

• Arrange strawberry slices in a spiral, starting from the outside and moving inward to reach the center. Push the tart up from the bottom, and let the side of the tart pan fall away.

• Slide the tart onto a platter and serve.

• Tart slices may be served over a small pool of frothy Sprouted Vanilla Almond Mylk or topped with a little Lemon Zing Frosting, and garnished with a sprinkle of bee pollen, if desired.

ROSEMARY CHILI PECANS

Makes 1½ cups

1½ cups raw pecans, soaked 6-8 hours, drained, and rinsed

1 Tbsp coconut nectar

2½ tsp minced fresh rosemary leaves

½ tsp red chili flakes

2 tsp tamari

2 tsp chia seeds

2-3 pinches salt

- In a medium mixing bowl, combine all ingredients and toss until well coated.
- On a dehydrator tray lined with a teflex sheet or parchment paper, spread the mixture in an even layer with a spatula.
- Dehydrate at 145°F for 2 hours to inhibit the growth of pathogens and rapidly reduce the moisture, then reduce temperature to 115°F and dehydrate for 4 more hours.
- Remove the teflex sheet or parchment paper so more air can circulate, and continue dehydrating at 115°F for 8 more hours, or until dry and crunchy.
- Serve immediately or store in a tightly sealed container at room temperature for up to 5 days, and include a desiccant packet.

SHISO GINGER PUMPKIN SEEDS

Makes 1 cup

¼ cup water

1 Tbsp chia seeds

1 cup raw pumpkin seeds, soaked 4-6 hours, drained, and rinsed

2 Tbsp minced Eden Foods Pickled Ginger with Shiso Leaves

1 Tbsp minced shallot

1 Tbsp tamari

¼ tsp salt

- In a small bowl, combine the water and chia seeds. Set aside to soak for about 30 minutes, or until it begins to gel.
- In a small mixing bowl, combine the chia gel with the remaining ingredients and stir until well mixed.
- On a dehydrator tray lined with a teflex sheet or parchment paper, spread the mixture in an even layer with a spatula.
- Follow remaining directions above for dehydrating and storing.

LEMONY DAMB SNACKIE THANGS

Makes 80-100 bite-size pieces

3-5 sheets nori, toasted or untoasted

½ cup nut mylk pulp (left over from
    the nut mylk–making process;
    pages 174, 177)

1⅓ oz yellow onion, chopped

⅔ oz flat-leaf parsley

⅓ oz basil leaves

¼ oz mint leaves

2 Tbsp lemon juice

1 Tbsp water

1 Tbsp olive oil

2 tsp nutritional yeast

1½ tsp dried dill weed

1 tsp tamari

½ tsp rubbed sage*

¼ tsp salt

¼ tsp freshly ground black pepper

3 Tbsp white sesame seeds, for garnish

- Trim the nori sheets into strips, then cut strips into squares. (Each sheet of nori should yield 25-30 squares.)
- In a food processor, combine all ingredients except the sesame seeds and pulse into a pâté.
- Using a fork, press a little morsel of the pâté into the center of 1 nori square (shiny side up), leaving little fork ridges for texture. Place nori square on a screened dehydrator tray. Repeat with remaining nori squares until all ingredients have been used, filling the whole dehydrator tray. Squares can be laid quite close together, even overlapped slightly. Garnish with sesame seeds.
- Dehydrate at 145°F for 2 hours to inhibit the growth of pathogens and rapidly reduce the moisture, then reduce temperature to 115°F and dehydrate for 12 more hours, or until crispy.
- Store up to 5-7 days in 1-2 glass jars with tight seals, and include a desiccant packet in each.

* If using ground dried sage, use about half the quantity specified.

DURING THE 2-HOUR PERIOD AT 145°F, THE FOOD TEMPERATURE IN THE DEHYDRATOR IS ABOUT 20-25°F COOLER, DUE TO THE RAPID EVAPORATION OF MOISTURE. MANY RAW-FOOD ENTHUSIASTS HAVE TESTED THIS METHOD AND FOUND THAT THE ENZYMES REMAIN VIABLE. DEHYDRATING AS DESCRIBED WILL REDUCE NOT ONLY THE RISK OF FERMENTATION AND PATHOGENS, IT WILL ALSO CUT OVERALL DRYING TIME AND PRODUCE A SUPERIOR PRODUCT.

ROASTED KALE CHIPS

Serves 2-4

1 head kale of choice, washed, dried,
    de-ribbed, torn into bite-size pieces

2 Tbsp olive oil

Spike Vegit Magic Gourmet Natural
    Seasoning

- Preheat the oven to 250°F. In a large mixing bowl, drizzle the oil over the kale and gently massage until all pieces have been coated. Sprinkle with Spike Vegit Magic seasoning to taste.
- On a baking tray lined with parchment paper, spread the kale pieces in an even layer. Roast for 20-25 minutes, or until crispy.
- Serve immediately or store in a tightly sealed container at room temperature for up to 5 days.

SPROUTED CHICKPEA HUMMUS

Experience sprouting in action with this refreshing hummus! But if there is not enough time to fully sprout the chickpeas, they can also be blended into hummus after just soaking. Serve with flaxseed crackers, roasted kale chips, or celery sticks. This can also be used as a salad topping, with One-Two Punch Balsamic Dressing (page 123).

Makes 2 cups

¾ cup dried chickpeas

2 cups water

½ cup red bell pepper, seeded and diced

3 Tbsp olive oil

¼ cup lemon juice

1½ cloves garlic, minced

1 tsp sea salt

1 tsp ground turmeric

• In a medium mixing bowl, place the dried chickpeas, cover with water, and set aside to soak for 12 hours. Drain and rinse the chickpeas, and transfer to a pan, covered with a towel so the chickpeas can breathe, and set aside overnight. In the morning, you should see little tails beginning to sprout!

• In a food processor, combine the sprouted chickpeas, red bell pepper, olive oil, lemon juice, garlic, salt, and turmeric, and puree for about 5 minutes, or until the mixture has a paste-like consistency.

• Leftover hummus can be stored in a tightly sealed container in the refrigerator for up to 5 days.

DEHYDRATING NUTS, SEEDS, GRAINS, VEGGIES, OR FRUITS AT LOW TEMPERATURES HELPS TO PRESERVE THE BENEFICIAL ENZYMES. FOR NUTS AND SEEDS ESPECIALLY, LOW-TEMP DEHYDRATION INSTEAD OF OVEN ROASTING ALSO PRESERVES THE INTEGRITY OF THEIR VOLATILE POLYUNSATURATED AND MONOUNSATURATED FATS, WHICH GO RANCID WHEN EXPOSED TO INTENSE HEAT AND LIGHT.

SMOKY LEMON HERB ALMONDS

Makes 1 cup

1 cup raw almonds, soaked 8-10 hours, drained, and rinsed

1 Tbsp lemon juice

1 Tbsp water

1½ tsp smoked sea salt

1 tsp lemon zest

½ tsp thyme leaves, minced

½ tsp rubbed sage*

¼ tsp freshly ground black pepper

¼ tsp white pepper

• In a medium mixing bowl, combine all ingredients and toss until well coated.

• On a dehydrator tray lined with a teflex sheet or parchment paper, spread the mixture in an even layer with a spatula.

• Dehydrate at 145°F for 2 hours to inhibit the growth of pathogens and rapidly reduce the moisture, then reduce the temperature to 115°F and dehydrate for 4 more hours.

• Remove the teflex sheet or parchment paper so more air can circulate, and continue dehydrating at 115°F for 8 more hours, or until dry and crunchy.

• Serve immediately or store in a tightly sealed container at room temperature for up to 5 days, and include a desiccant packet.

7

SMOOTHiES
& TONICS

BRIGHT EYES DANDELION JUICE

This is a strong medicinal drink. If feeling especially daring, try adding another inch of ginger to increase the potency. If feeling more timid, feel free to dilute it with a little more water.

Makes 1 quart

1-inch piece fresh ginger, peeled and cut into chunks

½ bunch (3 oz) dandelion greens

1 big handful (½ oz) kale

2 green apples, cored and cut into chunks

1 large (11 oz) cucumber, peeled and cut into chunks

1 stalk (2 oz) fennel, cut into chunks

1 cup water

Juice of 2 lemons

• With a juicer, first juice the ginger. Alternate juicing the greens, a little at a time, with chunks of the apple, cucumber, and fennel. Pour juice into a 1-quart jar and set aside.

• Pour the water through the juicer to flush out all the green goodness. Pour the rinse water into the juice jar, add lemon juice, and stir. Transfer to a glass and serve.

• If not consumed all at once, the remainder of this drink be stored in the refrigerator for up to 1 day. However, if this drink is being used to treat skin or tissue inflammation, it's best to drink the whole quart within a 2-to-3-hour period.

THE PRIMARY ORGAN OF DETOXIFICATION AND BLOOD FILTRATION, THE LIVER REMOVES TOXINS FROM THE BLOODSTREAM, INCLUDING EXCESS HORMONES. WHEN STRESSED OUT, THE BODY MANUFACTURES AN ABUNDANCE OF CORTISOL, WHICH HAS A DETRIMENTAL EFFECT ON MOOD AND THE IMMUNE SYSTEM AND CAN CREATE INSULIN RESISTANCE, LEADING TO ELEVATED BLOOD SUGAR LEVELS AND GENERAL INFLAMMATION. LACK OF SLEEP, CAFFEINE OVERCONSUMPTION, INFECTIONS, TRAUMA, OVEREXERTION, AND EXCESSIVE ALCOHOL ALL CONTRIBUTE TO ELEVATED CORTISOL LEVELS. AMAZINGLY, DANCING, LAUGHING, MUSIC, MASSAGE, MODERATE EXERCISE, MAGNESIUM, OMEGA-3 FATTY ACIDS, ASHWAGANDA, AND VITAMIN C ALL CONTRIBUTE DIRECTLY TO A REDUCTION IN CORTISOL, AS DO ADAPTOGENIC HERBS AND ANY SUBSTANCE THAT TONIFIES LIVER FUNCTION.

DANDELION HAS ANTI-INFLAMMATORY PROPERTIES, DUE IN PART TO ITS CAPACITY TO BOOST THE LIVER'S DETOXIFYING PROCESS. THE HEALTH OF THE LIVER IS REFLECTED IN THE EYES, SUCH AS YELLOWED WHITES, FROWN LINES, DRY EYE, OR "CHOLESTEROL BUMPS" ON THE EYELIDS OR UNDER-EYE AREA. CONSUMING FOODS THAT BOOST LIVER FUNCTION, SUCH AS DANDELION, NETTLES, SCHIZANDRA, AND TART CITRUS FRUITS, HELPS BRIGHTEN THE EYES.

SCHIZANDRA SMOOTHIE

This smoothie has special healing, beautifying properties due to the presence of dandelion, whose Latin name, *Taraxacum officinale,* means "remedy for disorder medicinal plant." Similarly, schizandra, a berry used in Chinese medicine, also boosts liver function, aids reproductive health, supports beautiful hair, skin, and nails, and is said to tonify all five organ systems with its unique flavor, which is simultaneously sweet, salty, sour, bitter, and spicy. Cold-pressed apple juice is recommended, as it is enzymatically active and contains the natural flavonoids and antioxidants.

Makes 1 quart, serves 1 as a breakfast

1 cup frozen blueberries

1 cup cold-pressed apple juice

1 cup water

1 lemon, peeled

1 small handful mixed greens

1 small handful
   dandelion greens

½ cup chopped cucumber

½ cup ice

½ avocado, cut into chunks

¼ cup chopped fennel bulb,
   stem, or fronds

2 tsp Billy's Infinity Greens

¼ tsp schizandra powder

¼ tsp ground vanilla beans
   or ½ tsp vanilla extract

8 drops liquid stevia

4 drops tangerine oil

- In a high-power blender, combine all ingredients and puree, first on low then gradually raising the speed to high, until smooth. Add an extra ¼ cup apple juice if a more traditional level of sweetness is desired.
- Transfer to a glass and serve.
- For a breakfast replacement, this can be consumed one pint at a time throughout the morning.

PEPPERMINT ICED MOCHA

Caffeine-free Dandy Blend tastes like coffee while providing the benefits of dandelion. The phenylethylamine (PEA) in cacao triggers the release of dopamine and norepinephrine in the brain, enhancing focus and increasing productivity. PEA also helps alleviate depression while promoting weight loss. Plant-based androgens in pine pollen support adrenal function, to regulate energy and balance hormones. Lion's mane supports memory, creativity, attention, and nerve regeneration, making it therapeutic for people with dementia, Parkinson's, MS, anxiety, depression, and cognitive impairment.

Serves 2

2 cups nut mylk
   (pages 174, 177)

2 Tbsp cacao powder

2-3 tsp Dandy Blend Instant
   Herbal Beverage

2 tsp raw honey

1 tsp pine pollen

1 tsp Om Lion's Mane
   mushroom powder

¼ tsp ground vanilla beans

5 drops liquid stevia

3 drops peppermint oil

- In a high-power blender, combine all ingredients and puree, first on low then gradually raising the speed to high, until frothy.
- Serve in ice-filled glasses.

BASIL HIBISCUS COOLER

Due to its high level of vitamin C, rose hip tea has long been used for immune support, but when combined with hibiscus, their conjoined antioxidant powers make this combo a cancer-fighting superhero. And that's not all—tea made from hibiscus flowers has also been shown to lower blood pressure and positively balance cholesterol and triglyceride levels. Honey boosted with a little stevia makes this beverage an enticing, low-sugar source of antioxidant hydration.

Makes about 8 cups

¼ oz dried hibiscus flowers

¼ oz dried rose hips

2 cups water, hot

6 cups water, cold

1 Tbsp raw honey

20 drops liquid stevia

7-8 basil leaves

- Soak hibiscus and rose hips in 2 cups hot water for 5-10 minutes until liquid is vividly colored, and pour through a strainer into a 2-quart glass jar with a tight seal.
- Add honey and stevia to the warm water, and shake to mix. Dilute with cold water.
- Serve chilled with fresh basil leaves.
- Can be stored in the refrigerator for up to 10 days.

CITRUS FENNEL BLASTER

The vitamin C in this beverage speaks volumes about the power of citrus to catalyze our immune function. There's a reason why we reach for vitamin C when feeling down: The liver loves tart citrus because it boosts its detoxifying powers. When fighting off a cold, the liver needs an extra citrus kick to help filter toxins from the bloodstream.

Makes 2½ cups

1-inch piece fresh ginger

1 grapefruit, peeled and cut into chunks

1 orange, peeled and cut into chunks

4½ oz fennel bulb, cut into chunks

4½ oz cucumber, peeled and cut into chunks

1 lemon, peeled and cut into chunks

1 lime, peeled and cut into chunks

- With a juicer, first juice the ginger, then all remaining ingredients.
- Transfer to a glass and serve.

8817
astragalus
ROOT

GOLDEN MYLK ASTRAGALUS LATTE

Serves 2

1½ cups water

3-inch piece ginger, peeled and thinly sliced

2-inch piece turmeric root, peeled and thinly sliced

2 Tbsp *or* 6 capsules astragalus root

6 cardamom pods

3 cinnamon sticks

¾ tsp ground turmeric

½ tsp ground clove

½ tsp black peppercorns

¼ tsp ground vanilla beans

1 pinch salt

1 dash ground cayenne

1½ cups Sprouted Brazil Nut Mylk (page 174)

1 tsp raw honey

3-4 drops liquid stevia

• In a small pot over medium heat, combine all ingredients except the Sprouted Brazil Nut Mylk, honey, and stevia, and bring to a boil. Reduce heat to low and simmer for 10 minutes.

• Remove from heat and strain contents into a high-power blender, add the remaining ingredients, and puree, first on low then gradually raising the speed to high, until frothy and well combined.

• Pour into glasses over ice, or gently reheat the mixture and serve in mugs.

WHILE THE CURCUMIN IN TURMERIC IS ONE OF THE MOST RESEARCHED AND STUDIED COMPOUNDS ON THE PLANET TODAY, HIGHLY REGARDED FOR ITS ANTI-INFLAMMATORY, ANTIDEPRESSANT, CHEMOPROTECTIVE, ANTICANCER, ANTICOAGULANT, AND PAIN-REDUCING HEALTH BENEFITS, ASTRAGALUS HAS BEEN WIDELY REVERED FOR THOUSANDS OF YEARS IN TRADITIONAL CHINESE MEDICINE AS ONE OF THE BEST ADAPTOGENS FOR SUPPORTING THE BODY DURING TIMES OF PHYSICAL, MENTAL, OR EMOTIONAL STRESS. CORTISOL- AND CHOLESTEROL-LOWERING, ASTRAGALUS HAS PROFOUND IMMUNE-BOOSTING PROPERTIES, DUE TO THE PRESENCE OF ANTIMICROBIAL, ANTIVIRAL, AND ANTI-INFLAMMATORY POLYSACCHARIDES; ASTRAGALUS ALSO HAS EXHIBITED CANCER-PREVENTIVE AND CHEMOPROTECTIVE PROPERTIES. GOLDEN MYLK ASTRAGALUS LATTE PROVIDES HEALTH BENEFITS FOR THE CIRCULATORY AND IMMUNE SYSTEMS AS WELL AS INFLAMMATION AND PAIN RELIEF; MAKING IT EXCELLENT TO CONSUME ANY TIME ONE IS FEELING BLUE, SLUGGISH, OR UNDER THE WEATHER.

GINGER PEAR SMOOTHIE

Makes 1 quart, serves 1 as a breakfast

1 pear, cored and cut into chunks

1 handful leafy greens

1 cup water

1 cup ice

1 lemon, peeled and cut
   into chunks

½ cup cucumber, chopped

½ avocado, peeled and cut into
   chunks

¼ cup chopped celery

2-inch piece fresh ginger, peeled
   and sliced

1 Tbsp flaxseed oil

1-2 tsp E3Live AFA Crystal Flakes

4 drops liquid stevia

• In a high-power blender, combine all ingredients
and blend until smooth.

• Transfer to a glass and serve.

• For a breakfast replacement, this can be consumed
one pint at a time throughout the morning.

DUE TO ITS HIGH CONCENTRATION OF BLUE-GREEN PIGMENTS, APHANIZOMENON FLOS-AQUAE, OR AFA, IS A SUPERCHARGED SOURCE OF CHLOROPHYLL, WHICH HAS MYRIAD HEALTH BENEFITS. AFA IS LOADED WITH 64 MICRONUTRIENTS, AND ITS NUCLEIC ACIDS STIMULATE THE IMMUNE SYSTEM, MIGRATING 40 PERCENT OF THE NATURAL KILLER CELLS (NKCs) FROM THE BLOOD INTO THE TISSUES.

PARSLEY LIME JING JUICE

Makes about 2 cups

4 stalks celery

1 green apple, peeled and cut
   into chunks

1 lime, peeled and cut
   into chunks

2-inch piece ginseng root

1 oz flat-leaf parsley, minced

½ cup water

• With a juicer, juice the celery, apple, lime, ginseng, and
parsley. Pour mixture into a 1-pint container and set aside.

• Pour the water through the juicer to flush out all the green
goodness. Pour rinse water into juice mixture and stir.

• Serve in glasses over ice.

AN ADAPTOGENIC ROOT, GINSENG HAS A LONG HISTORY IN CHINESE MEDICINE, AND WAS ONCE WORTH ITS WEIGHT IN GOLD TO CHINESE EMPERORS. ITS LATIN NAME, PANAX, COMES FROM THE GREEK FOR "ALL HEALING," AND IT SUPPORTS THE BODY WITH ENERGY-BOOSTING PROPERTIES TO INCREASE MENTAL AND PHYSICAL ENDURANCE. GINSENG IS GREAT FOR A VARIETY OF AILMENTS FROM ALZHEIMER'S TO GOUT.

EMERALD JULIUS SMOOTHIE

Experience the metabolism-boosting benefits of fasting three to five days a week with a green smoothie for breakfast.

Makes 1 quart, serves 1 as a breakfast

1 large Valencia orange, peeled

1 big handful mixed greens

1 cup No Excuses Nut Mylk
  (page 174)

1 cup ice

1 lemon, peeled and cut into chunks

4-inch stalk celery, chopped

¼ avocado, cut into chunks

1½-inch piece cucumber

2 Tbsp almond butter

2 Tbsp Billy's Infinity Protein powder

1 Tbsp flaxseed oil

2 tsp Billy's Infinity Greens

1-2 tsp DeSouza's Liquid Chlorophyll

1 tsp raw honey

¼ tsp ground vanilla beans

4-5 drops liquid stevia

THIS SMOOTHIE DELIVERS 25 GRAMS OF PLANT-BASED PROTEIN. THE ANTIOXIDANT-RICH CHLOROPHYLL AND PHYCOCYANINS FROM THE ALGAE IN BILLY'S INFINITY GREENS AND THE LEAFY VEGETABLES IN THIS SMOOTHIE ARE A POWERFUL INTERNAL DEODORANT AND A MINERAL-RICH SOURCE OF IMMUNE-STIMULATING NUTRITION.

• In a high-power blender, combine all ingredients and puree, first on low then gradually raising the speed to high, until well mixed.

• Transfer to a glass and serve.

• For a breakfast replacement, this can be consumed 1 pint at a time throughout the morning.

NOTE TO THE CALORIE-CONSCIOUS: FATS LIKE AVOCADO, FLAXSEED OIL, AND RAW ALMOND BUTTER ARE NOT FATTENING, THEY ARE SATIATING. IN FACT, THESE FATS ARE ESSENTIAL FOR REDUCING INFLAMMATION AND BALANCING TRIGLYCERIDES. FURTHERMORE, THE CALORIES FROM SUGARS IN THIS SMOOTHIE COME FROM 1 WHOLE ORANGE, 1 WHOLE LEMON, AND 1 TEASPOON OF RAW HONEY. NATURAL SUGARS TAKEN IN THEIR WHOLE FORMAT ARE PROCESSED AND UTILIZED VERY DIFFERENTLY BY THE BODY THAN THE SUGAR CALORIES IN A SOFT DRINK OR A PASTRY. THE 1:1 RATIO OF FRUCTOSE TO GLUCOSE IN HONEY IS EASILY PROCESSED BY THE LIVER, ALLOWING IT TO ENTER THE BLOODSTREAM ALMOST IMMEDIATELY WITH A LOWER GLYCEMIC RESPONSE, MAKING IT AN IDEAL FOOD FOR ATHLETES. HONEY ALSO IS A PERFECT FUEL FOR THE BRAIN, TO REDUCE METABOLIC STRESS AND PROMOTE RESTFUL SLEEP, AND STUDIES SHOW THAT HONEY MAY ALSO HELP PREVENT COGNITIVE DECLINE. BASING SMOOTHIES IN GREENS, AVOCADO, AND NON-STARCHY VEGETABLES LIKE CELERY AND CUCUMBER IS A GREAT WAY TO ADD MORE FRESH FIBER TO THE DIET. A SMOOTHIE LIKE THIS WILL PROMOTE REGULARITY, STIMULATE METABOLISM, AND BOOST THE LIVER'S DETOX PROCESS.

PINEAPPLE CILANTRO LIME COOLER

Makes 1 quart

¼ pineapple, cut into chunks

1 medium cucumber, peeled and cut into chunks

2½ cups water

Juice of 4-5 limes

½ tsp minced fresh cilantro

- With a juicer, juice the pineapple and cucumber. Pour into a 1-quart jar.
- Add the water, lime juice, and cilantro to the jar. Seal and shake well to combine.
- Serve in glasses over ice.

THIS ELECTROLYTE TONIC FEATURES THE PROTEOLYTIC ENZYMES EREPSIN AND BROMELAIN. PINEAPPLE AND CUCUMBER HAVE ANTI-INFLAMMATORY PROPERTIES, AND CUCUMBER IS WELL KNOWN FOR ITS COOLING PROPERTIES. AS AN ACIDIC FRUIT, LIME PRODUCES AN ALKALINE RESPONSE WITHIN THE BODY.

CARROT APPLE LIME COOLER

This drink can be made with the carrot and apple juice reserved from the 24-Carrot Birthday Cake recipe (page 126).

Makes about 2 cups

8 medium carrots, peeled and cut into chunks

2 green apples, peeled and cut into chunks

¾ cup water

Juice of 3-4 limes

- With a juicer, juice the carrots and apples. Pour into a 1-quart jar.
- Add the water and lime juice. Seal and shake well to combine.
- Transfer to a glass and serve.

MACA MUSHROOM CHAI MYLK ICED LATTE

This concoction makes a fantastic low-caffeine afternoon pick-me-up.

Serves 2

3 cups No Excuses Nut Mylk (page 174)

1 Tbsp Billy's Infinity Chai

1 Tbsp fresh ginger, peeled and chopped

1 tsp gelatinized maca root powder

½ tsp freshly ground black pepper

1-2 capsules ashwaganda root

2 dashes ground cardamom

5 drops liquid stevia

• In a high-power blender, combine 1 cup of No Excuses Nut Mylk with all other ingredients, and puree, first on low then gradually raising the speed to high, until well mixed.

• Dilute mixture with the remaining 2 cups nut mylk and blend again until light and frothy.

• Serve in ice-filled glasses.

REFERRED TO AS "STRENGTH OF THE STALLION," ASHWAGANDA IS AN INCREDIBLE ADAPTOGENIC HERB THAT CAN HELP COMBAT STRESS BY LOWERING CORTISOL LEVELS, BOOSTING IMMUNITY, IMPROVING THYROID FUNCTION, AND ADDRESSING ADRENAL FATIGUE. IN BILLY'S INFINITY CHAI THERE ARE MANY MEDICINAL MUSHROOMS, BUT CORDYCEPS IN PARTICULAR IS WELL KNOWN FOR IMPROVING ATHLETIC ENDURANCE, BOOSTING ENERGY, AND MITIGATING ADRENAL FATIGUE. MACA ALSO BOASTS ADAPTOGENIC PROPERTIES RELATED TO REGULATING REPRODUCTIVE HORMONES. THE USE OF MACA BY NATIVE PERUVIANS FOR NUTRITIONAL AND MEDICINAL PURPOSES PREDATES THE INCAS, WITH PRIMITIVE CULTIVATION DATING BACK TO 1600 B.C. REVERED FOR ITS FERTILITY- AND STAMINA-INDUCING PROPERTIES, IT WAS PAID AS A TRIBUTE TO THE SPANISH BY THE CONQUERED INCAS IN THE 1500s, AND THE SPANISH FED IT TO THEIR TROOPS TO INCREASE THEIR VITALITY AND FORTITUDE. WHEN THE SPANIARDS VENTURED INTO THE HIGH ALTITUDES OF THE ANDES, THEY FOUND THE STRESS TOO PHYSICALLY TAXING FOR THEM AND THEIR LIVESTOCK, WHO WERE NOT REPRODUCING WELL. TAKING A CUE FROM THE INDIGENOUS ANDEANS, THE SPANIARDS BEGAN EATING MACA AND FEEDING IT TO THEIR ANIMALS AS WELL. THE EFFECTS OF MACA ON BOTH MAN AND BEAST WERE SO STARTLING, THE CONQUISTADORS SOON DEMANDED TO BE PAID IN MACA INSTEAD OF GOLD.

ALOE BLUEBERRY TWIST

A well-known adaptogen, aloe vera has anti-inflammatory, antibacterial, antifungal, and antiviral properties. Its topical benefits for treating sunburns and rashes are well known, but it can also be taken internally. Aloe vera can have a profound laxative effect if more than 3-4 ounces are ingested, therefore large amounts of aloe vera are not recommended for pregnant women, or people with diabetes, thyroid, or kidney conditions.

Serves 1

2 oz fresh aloe vera leaves, cut into chunks

1 oz fresh mint leaves

1 stalk celery, cut into chunks

1 green apple, cored and cut into chunks

½ large cucumber, cut into chunks

½ cup water

⅓ cup frozen wild blueberries

Juice of 1 lemon

¼ tsp schizandra powder

• With a juicer, first juice the aloe leaves, followed by the mint, celery, green apple, and cucumber. Pour mixture into a large serving glass and set aside.
• Pour the water through the juicer to flush out all the green goodness.
• Transfer the rinse water to a blender, add the blueberries, lemon juice, and schizandra, and blend until smooth and deep purple in color.
• Gently pour purple berry mixture into the glass with the green juice, to create a stunning two-tone drink.

WHAT MAKES BLUEBERRIES BLUE? THE DEEP PIGMENTS FOUND IN THE SKIN OF BLUEBERRIES ARE FLAVONOIDS CALLED ANTHOCYANINS, WHICH DEVELOP IN RESPONSE TO SUNLIGHT. THESE ARE SOME OF THE MOST STABLE ANTIOXIDANTS KNOWN, BLEEDING THEMSELVES DRY OF PIGMENT AS THEY RESOLVE FREE-RADICAL DAMAGE. THE ORAC (OXYGEN RADICAL ABSORBANCE CAPACITY) VALUE FOR BLUEBERRIES IS SIGNIFICANT, BUT WILD BLUEBERRIES TAKE IT TO ANOTHER LEVEL. NATIVE TO NORTH AMERICA, WILD BLUEBERRIES ARE A SUPREME WILD SUPERFOOD. CLOCKING IN AT A WHOPPING 9600 ORAC UNITS PER 100 GRAMS, WILD BLUEBERRIES HAVE TWICE AS MUCH ANTIOXIDANT POWER AS DOMESTIC BLUEBERRIES (A MERE 4700 UNITS, WHICH IS STILL QUITE HIGH!), AND THE DIFFERENCE IS PLAIN TO SEE. USING PLUMP DOMESTIC BLUEBERRIES FOR SMOOTHIES AND TONICS WILL MAKE THEM MOMENTARILY PURPLE, BUT THE COLOR QUICKLY FADES TO GRAY. WILD BLUEBERRIES, HOWEVER, PROVIDE RICH PURPLE ANTIOXIDANT COLORING TO YOUR SMOOTHIES, TONICS, AND TREATS THAT LASTS. IN ADDITION TO FIGHTING FREE RADICALS, WILD BLUEBERRIES ARE ALSO RENOWNED FOR THEIR ANTI-INFLAMMATORY PROPERTIES, AND ARE BENEFICIAL FOR THE HEART, BRAIN, URINARY TRACT, GUT, AND METABOLISM.

BLACK FOREST SMOOTHIE

Raw cacao is one of the most antioxidant-rich foods on earth, containing about 96,000 ORAC (Oxygen Radical Absorbance Capacity) units per 100 grams. The antioxidant pigments found in raw cacao, like those found in other vibrant or deeply colored fruits and vegetables, are particularly stable when it comes to protecting cells from lesions caused by free radicals.

Makes 1 quart, serves 1 as a breakfast

2 cups Sprouted Vanilla Almond Mylk (page 177)
1 cup frozen black cherries
½ cup diced cucumber
1 handful leafy greens
2 oz young coconut meat
2½ Tbsp raw cacao powder
1 Tbsp flaxseed oil
1 tsp Om Cordyceps mushroom powder
½ tsp chocolate extract
¼ tsp ground vanilla beans
4-6 drops liquid stevia

- In a blender, combine all ingredients and blend until smooth, and serve in a glass.
- For a breakfast replacement, this can be consumed one pint at a time throughout the morning.

CHOCO CHIA SMOOTHIE

Known as "the mushroom of immortality," reishi has been extensively studied and found to stimulate the immune system, aid in cancer prevention, and support overall longevity. However, it should not be taken every day over an extended period. Try taking reishi for a few weeks, then switch to some other superfoods or medicinal mushrooms, to cultivate moderation in all things.

Makes 1 quart, serves 1 as a breakfast

⅓ cup water
1 Tbsp chia seeds
2 cups Sprouted Vanilla Almond Mylk (page 177)
1 big handful greens
1 Persian cucumber, cut into chunks
1 cup sliced frozen banana
3 Tbsp raw cacao powder
1 Tbsp Billy's Infinity Protein powder
1 tsp maca root powder
½ tsp Om Reishi mushroom powder
½ tsp chocolate extract
¼ tsp ground vanilla beans, or ½ tsp vanilla extract

- In a small bowl, combine the water and chia seeds. Set aside to soak for 20-30 minutes, or until it begins to gel.
- In a high-power blender, combine all other ingredients and puree, first on low then gradually raising the speed to high, until well mixed. Add the chia seeds and soaking water and blend again on low until just combined.
- Serve in a glass, over ice, if desired.
- For a breakfast replacement, this can be consumed one pint at a time throughout the morning.

8

CHEEZES, MYLKS, DRESSINGS & SAUCES

BASIL OIL DRESSING

Makes about ½ cup, serves 4-6

⅙ oz fresh basil leaves

⅓ cup olive oil

2 Tbsp white wine vinegar

1 Tbsp lemon juice

3 pinches sea salt and freshly
   ground black pepper

- In a blender or a food processor, combine the basil and oil and pulse on low just until the oil turns green (do not overblend, or the oil will turn brown). Gently strain the mixture through a nut mylk bag to remove the basil pulp.
- Transfer to a glass jar with a tight seal. Add the remaining ingredients, seal, and shake to mix.
- Use immediately or store in the refrigerator for up to 5 days.

THREE-SEED CINNAMON MYLK

Makes about 6 cups

⅓ cup raw pumpkin seeds

⅓ cup hulled sesame seeds

⅓ cup raw sunflower seeds

Water, as needed, for soaking

1 Tbsp ground cinnamon

¼ tsp ground vanilla beans

10-15 drops liquid stevia,
   to taste

1 pinch sea salt

5 cups water

- Combine all seeds in a bowl and cover with water. Set aside to soak 4-6 hours.
- Place a very fine screen over the top of the bowl to drain and rinse the seeds without losing any.
- In a high-power blender, add the seeds and enough water to reach the 2½-cup line, and puree until smooth and creamy; the mixture will be very thick. Add water to the 5-cup line and blend again.
- Strain the mixture through a nut mylk bag and save the leftover pulp for other snacks and treats (pages 38, 137, 144).
- Transfer the mylk to a glass jar with a tight seal. Add the cinnamon, vanilla, and stevia and shake to mix.
- Use immediately or seal and store in the refrigerator for up to 4 days.

LITTLE SEEDS SUCH AS SUNFLOWER, SESAME, AND PUMPKIN ARE RICH IN PROTEIN, ESSENTIAL FATTY ACIDS, AND MINERAL NUTRITION. SESAME IS A SOURCE OF CALCIUM, PUMPKIN SEEDS ARE LOADED WITH ZINC AND BENEFICIAL FOR PROSTATE HEALTH, WHILE THE SUNFLOWER SEED IS ABUNDANT IN MAGNESIUM. THESE SEEDS ARE ALSO ABUNDANT IN PHYTOSTEROLS, WHICH PROMOTE HEALTHY CHOLESTEROL LEVELS.

GINGER BEET SUNFLOWER SEED CHEEZE PÂTÉ

This pâté becomes a satisfying meal when served over lettuce leaves with sliced avocado, celery sticks, and cucumber wedges, along with slices of toasted manna bread or dehydrated vegetable or seed crackers, and drizzled with Ginger Flax Dressing (page 179).

Makes 3 cups

3 cups raw sunflower seeds, soaked 4-6 hours, drained, and rinsed

1 Tbsp unpasteurized white miso

4 cups water

¾ cup beets, peeled and shredded

¾ cup carrots, peeled and shredded

¼ cup onion, minced

¼ cup flat-leaf parsley, chopped

¼ cup cilantro, chopped

2 Tbsp Bragg Liquid Aminos

1 Tbsp nutritional yeast

1 Tbsp sesame seeds

1 Tbsp flaxseed oil

1-inch piece ginger, peeled and grated

1 small clove garlic, minced

¼ tsp hot pepper–toasted sesame oil

5 Tbsp lemon juice

Lettuce leaves, avocado slices, celery sticks, cucumber wedges, toasted manna bread, and/or crackers, for serving (optional)

• In a high-power blender, combine sunflower seeds, miso, and water, and puree into a fine slurry, but not a cream.

• Transfer the mixture to 2-quart jars with lids and cover them with screen lids or some cheesecloth. Set the jars in a warm place (e.g., the top of your refrigerator) and let it ferment for 6-12 hours, until the pulp has separated from the fluid and little bubbles have formed. Technically, it can go longer—up to 24 hours—but this will produce a stronger smelling mixture. (If the mixture has fermented long enough and you don't have time to squeeze it, you can seal the lids and refrigerate it for up to a day, to slow the fermentation process.)

• Strain the mixture, 1 cup at a time, through a nut mylk bag, squeezing out and discarding the liquid. If it feels a little tingly, that means the probiotics are alive and kicking.

• Transfer the dry, crumbly bits to a mixing bowl. Without stirring, add the beets, carrots, onion, parsley, cilantro, Bragg Liquid Aminos, yeast, sesame seeds, flaxseed oil, ginger, garlic, and sesame oil in separate piles.

• Pour the lemon juice directly over the pile of beets and nothing else. This will cause them to bleed all over the seed cheeze, turning it a lovely bright pink color.

• Gently mash ingredients into a tabouleh-like mixture and serve alone or with a green salad, or press it into a form and use as a spread or dip for crackers, toast, vegetable sticks, as desired.

BRAZIL NUT SUNSHINE SALAD

Makes about 3½ cups, serves 4-8

½ cup raw brazil nuts, soaked
   12 hours, drained, and rinsed

1 Tbsp unpasteurized white miso

Water, as needed

¾ cup yellow or orange
   bell pepper, diced

¼ cup onion, diced

3 Tbsp cilantro, chopped

2½ Tbsp lemon juice

1-2 Tbsp mint leaves, chiffonaded

1 Tbsp nutritional yeast

1 tsp Bragg Liquid Aminos

1 tsp lemon zest

1 tsp sesame oil

½ tsp salt

¼ tsp white pepper

1 tsp turmeric powder,
   or the juice of a 4-inch piece
   fresh turmeric root and
   1 small carrot

• In a high-power blender, combine the brazil nuts, miso, and enough water to cover by 1 inch and blend into a fine meal, but not a cream.

• Transfer the mixture to a 1-quart jar with a lid and cover it with a screen or some cheesecloth. Set the jar in a warm place (e.g., the top of the refrigerator) and let it ferment for 8-12 hours, until the pulp has separated from the fluid and little bubbles have formed. Technically, it can go longer—up to 24 hours—but this will produce a stronger smelling nut pulp. (If the nut pulp has fermented long enough and you don't have time to squeeze it, you can seal the lid and refrigerate it for up to a day, to slow the fermentation process.)

• Strain the mixture, 1 cup at a time, through a nut mylk bag, squeezing out and discarding the liquid. If the nut pulp smells strong, you can rinse it inside the bag with more fresh water and squeeze out the moisture.

• Transfer the dry, crumbly bits to a large mixing bowl. Add the bell pepper, onion, cilantro, lemon juice, mint, yeast, Bragg Liquid Aminos, zest, oil, salt, and white pepper and gently mash. For color, add the turmeric. Gently fold all ingredients together until the salad takes on a sunny yellow color.

• Serve immediately or transfer to a glass jar with a tight seal and store in the refrigerator for up to 4 days.

TURMERIC—THE SUNNY YELLOW INGREDIENT THAT GIVES CURRY POWDER ITS VIBRANT COLOR—IS ALL THE RAGE THESE DAYS, BUT ITS MEDICINAL PROPERTIES HAVE BEEN WELL KNOWN FOR CENTURIES. PERHAPS THE MOST POTENT COMPOUND IN TURMERIC IS CURCUMIN, WHICH HAS BEEN EXPLORED IN OVER 6,000 PEER-REVIEWED ARTICLES. THE CONSENSUS IS THAT CURCUMIN RIVALS OR BEATS PRESCRIPTION MEDICATIONS IN TREATING A WIDE RANGE OF CONDITIONS INCLUDING INFLAMMATION, ARTHRITIS, IBS, HEART DISEASE, CANCER, VASCULAR THROMBOSIS, LIVER DISEASE, PAIN, AND EVEN DEPRESSION, SUPPORTING THE CONTENTION THAT EATING AN ANTIOXIDANT RAINBOW OF RICHLY PIGMENTED FRESH FOODS IS A POWERFUL MEANS TO STAY HEALTHY AND HAPPY.

GOJI TOMATO CHILI PASTE

This recipe is excellent on Eggie Tacos (page 28), with Macadamia Ricotta (page 182), or with anything else you want to spice up.

Makes about 1¼ cups
½ cup warm water
1 chipotle pepper, seeded,
    or 1 tsp chipotle powder
3 Tbsp goji berries
1¼ oz sundried tomatoes
1½ Tbsp raw honey

2-inch piece fresh ginger,
    peeled and sliced
¼ cup flaxseed oil
2 tsp apple cider vinegar
¾ tsp smoked sea salt
1 small clove garlic,
    smashed

GOJI BERRIES HAVE LONG BEEN ASSOCIATED WITH LONGEVITY, VASCULAR HEALTH, AND MENTAL ALERTNESS, BUT ARE CONTRAINDICATED WHEN TAKING THE DRUG WARFARIN OR MEDICATIONS FOR BLOOD PRESSURE OR DIABETES.

• In a high-power blender, combine water, chipotle pepper, goji berries, and sundried tomatoes, and set aside to soak for about 20 minutes, or until they begin to soften (do not discard the soaking water).
• Add the remaining ingredients and puree, first on low then gradually raising the speed to high, until smooth.
• Use immediately or transfer to a glass jar with a tight seal and store in the refrigerator for up to 1 week.

SUPER YUM DRESSING

Makes about 1½ cups
⅔ cup red bell pepper,
    cut into chunks
⅓ cup water
¼ cup lemon juice
¼ cup raw pine nuts,
    soaked 4-6 hours,
    drained, and rinsed
¼ cup raw macadamia
    nuts, soaked 8 hours,
    drained, and rinsed

2 Tbsp almond butter
2 Tbsp nutritional yeast
1 Tbsp flaxseed oil
1 Tbsp olive oil
2 tsp Bragg Liquid Aminos
1 tsp ume plum vinegar
½ tsp smoked paprika
½ tsp ground chipotle

• In a high-power blender, combine all ingredients and puree, first on low then gradually raising the speed to high, until smooth and creamy.
• Use immediately or transfer to a glass jar with a tight seal and store in refrigerator for up to 1 week.

NO EXCUSES NUT MYLK

Makes 4-6 cups

3 Tbsp raw pine nuts, soaked
   4-6 hours, drained, and rinsed

¼ cup raw almond butter

¼ tsp ground vanilla beans

6-8 drops liquid stevia*

4-6 cups water

* For sweeter nut mylk,
add 1-2 tsp raw honey.

• In a high-power blender, combine pine nuts, almond butter, vanilla, stevia, and 1 cup of water and puree, first on low then gradually raising the speed to high, until the mixture is very smooth.

• Add water to any point between the 4-6 cup lines on the blender, to reach desired level of creaminess. Puree, first on low then gradually raising the speed to high, until well mixed. Strain through a nut mylk bag and save the leftover pulp for other snacks and treats (pages 38, 137, 144).

• Transfer to a glass jar with a tight seal. Store in the refrigerator for up to 4 days.

SPROUTED BRAZIL NUT MYLK

Makes about 4 cups

⅔ cup raw brazil nuts, soaked
   8-12 hours, drained,
   and rinsed

1 pinch sea salt

4 drops liquid stevia*

4 cups water

* For sweeter nut mylk,
add 1-2 tsp raw honey.

• In a high-power blender, combine brazil nuts, salt, stevia, and 1 cup of water and puree, first on low then gradually raising the speed to high, until creamy and well mixed.

• Dilute with the remaining 3 cups of water, to just above the 4-cup line. Blend again on high until frothy and well mixed.

• Strain mixture through a nut mylk bag and save the leftover pulp for other snacks and treats (pages 38, 137, 144).

• Use immediately or transfer to a glass jar with a tight seal and store in the refrigerator up to 4 days.

SPROUTED WALNUT MYLK

Makes about 4 cups

4 cups water

⅔ cup raw walnuts, soaked 8-12 hours, drained, and rinsed

1 pinch sea salt

4 drops liquid stevia*

* For sweeter nut mylk, add 1-2 tsp raw honey.

- In a high-power blender, combine 1 cup water, the walnuts, salt, and stevia and puree, first on low then gradually raising the speed to high, until the mixture is creamy.
- Dilute with more water to the 4-cup line. Blend on high until frothy and well mixed.
- Strain mixture through a nut mylk bag and save the leftover pulp for other snacks and treats (pages 38, 137, 144).
- Use immediately or transfer to a glass jar with a tight seal and store in the refrigerator for up to 4 days.

SPROUTED VANILLA ALMOND MYLK

Makes about 4 cups

4½ cups water

½ cup raw almonds, soaked 8-12 hours, drained, and rinsed

½ tsp vanilla extract

¼ tsp ground vanilla beans

1 pinch sea salt

6-8 drops liquid stevia*

* For sweeter nut mylk, add 1-2 tsp raw honey.

- In a high-power blender, combine 2 cups water, the almonds, vanilla extract and beans, salt, and stevia and puree, first on low then gradually raising the speed to high, until mixture is creamy.
- Dilute with more water to the 4½-cup line. Blend on high until frothy and well mixed.
- Strain mixture through a nut mylk bag and save the leftover pulp for other snacks and treats (pages 38, 137, 144).
- Use immediately or transfer to a glass jar with a tight seal and store in the refrigerator for up to 4 days.

GINGER FLAX DRESSING

Makes about 1 cup

6 Tbsp flaxseed oil

5 Tbsp lemon juice

2 Tbsp tamari

2 Tbsp finely grated
fresh ginger

1 Tbsp Bragg Liquid
Aminos

1½ Tbsp coconut nectar

2 tsp hot sesame oil

1 tsp ume plum vinegar

- Combine all ingredients in a glass jar, seal, and shake to mix.
- Use immediately or store in the refrigerator for up to 2 weeks.

GINGER IS A POTENT ANTINAUSEA BOTANICAL FoR UPSET STOMACH, DRAMATICALLY iMPROVING THE DIGESTIVE PROCESS AND BOOSTING METABOLISM. ITS SPICY TASTE BELIES ITS INCREDIBLE ANTI-INFLAMMATORY PROPERTIES, WHICH ACCORDING TO CHINESE MEDICINE EXPELS WIND AND COLD FROM THE LUNGS AND LARGE INTESTINE, THEREBY TONIFYING THESE RELATED ORGANS.

CHIMICHURRI

Makes about 2 cups

1½ cups flat-leaf parsley,
finely minced

1 cup olive oil

3 cloves garlic, minced

2 Tbsp red wine vinegar

1 Tbsp lemon juice

1½ tsp red chili flakes

1 tsp sea salt

½ tsp freshly ground
black pepper

½ tsp fresh oregano
leaves, minced

- In a mixing bowl, add all ingredients and stir until well combined.
- Use immediately or transfer to a glass jar with a tight seal and store in the refrigerator for up to 5 days.

WALNUT HERB-CRUSTED CROQUETTES

Serve over a bed of greens with roasted vegetables (pages 100, 110, 115, 120, 123), or as part of a cheeze plate with crackers and fresh veggie spears.

Makes 6 croquettes

¼ cup raw walnuts

2 Tbsp flat-leaf parsley, minced

1 Tbsp dried basil

¼ tsp rubbed sage*

1 pinch dried tarragon

¾ cup Macadamia Ricotta (page 182)

* If using ground dried sage, use about half the quantity specified.

- In a food processor, add the walnuts and pulse into a fine meal. Add the herbs and gently pulse a few more times until well mixed. Transfer to a small bowl.
- Scoop 2 Tbsp dollops of Macadamia Ricotta and form them into little patties. Gently dredge the patties in the walnut mixture and lightly press to evenly coat.
- Transfer croquettes to a dehydrator set at 110°F for 6 hours, *or* to a 150°F oven for 20-30 minutes, until warm and crisp.

CILANTRO DE GALLO SALSA

Makes 1½ cups

4 roma tomatoes, diced

⅓ cup cilantro, finely chopped

¼ cup red onion, diced

Juice of 1 lime

¼ tsp sea salt

2-3 pinches freshly ground black pepper

3 dashes ground chipotle

- Combine all ingredients in a small bowl and stir until well combined.
- Use immediately or store in a glass jar with a tight seal in the refrigerator for up to 5 days.

GRIND YOUR OWN CHIPOTLE POWDER IN A COFFEE/SPICE GRINDER FROM WHOLE PEPPERS.

MACADAMIA RICOTTA

Can be served as a spread, dolloped on salads or pizzas, or baked on top of egg dishes.

Makes 1½ cups

1 cup raw macadamia nuts,
   soaked 8 hours, drained,
   and rinsed
¼ cup raw pine nuts, soaked
   8 hours, drained, and rinsed
9 raw brazil nuts, soaked
   8 hours, drained, and rinsed
¼ cup raw cashews, soaked
   8 hours, drained, and rinsed
1 Tbsp unpasteurized white miso
Water, as needed
6 Tbsp Sprouted Walnut Mylk
   (page 177) *or* water
¼ cup lemon juice
1 Tbsp nutritional yeast
1 tsp dried onion flakes
½ tsp Bragg Liquid Aminos
½ tsp salt

• In a high-power blender, combine all nuts, miso, and enough water to cover by 1 inch and blend into a fine meal, but not a cream.
• Transfer mixture to a 1-quart jar with a lid and cover it with a screen lid or some cheesecloth. Set the jar in a warm place (e.g., the top of your refrigerator) and let it ferment for 8-12 hours, until the pulp has separated from the fluid and little bubbles have formed. Technically, it can go longer—up to 24 hours—but this will produce a stronger-smelling nut pulp. (If the nut pulp has fermented long enough and you don't have time to squeeze it, you can seal the lid and refrigerate it for up to a day, to slow the fermentation process.)
• Strain the mixture, 1 cup at a time, through a nut mylk bag, squeezing out and discarding the liquid. If the nut pulp smells strong, you can rinse it inside the bag with more fresh water and squeeze out the moisture.
• Transfer the dry, crumbly bits to a food processor. Add the Sprouted Walnut Mylk *or* water, lemon juice, yeast, onion flakes, Bragg Liquid Aminos, and salt and pulse for several minutes, until it takes on a smooth, ricotta-like consistency.
• Use immediately or transfer to a glass jar with a tight seal and store in the refrigerator for up to 4 days.

FERMENTED FOODS PLAY A CRUCIAL ROLE IN THE BALANCE OF OUR INNER ECOLOGY, NAMELY THE MICROBIOME OF FRIENDLY PROBIOTICS IN THE GUT. IT IS RECOMMENDED TO CONSUME A MINIMUM OF 10 BILLION NEW COLONY-FORMING UNITS (CFUS) PER DAY. THIS CAN BE IN THE FORM OF PROBIOTIC CAPSULES OR A FEW SPOONFULS OF FERMENTED WHOLE FOODS SUCH AS SAUERKRAUT, KIMCHI, YOGURT, KEFIR, FERMENTED SALSAS, AND SO ON. A HEALTHY GROUP OF PROBIOTICS PRODUCES 95 PERCENT OF THE SEROTONIN IN THE BODY, CRITICAL FOR MAINTAINING A POSITIVE MOOD AND PERSEVERANCE IN CHALLENGING SITUATIONS.

MEXICAN MOLÉ SAUCE

Makes about 3 cups, serves 4-10

1 dried ancho chili

1 dried pasilla chili

1 Tbsp dried cranberries

1 Tbsp coconut oil

½ yellow onion, diced

2 cloves garlic, minced

1 Tbsp raw macadamia nuts

1 Tbsp black sesame seeds

1 Tbsp raw pumpkin seeds

¼ tsp chipotle powder

1 tsp cumin seeds
   or ground cumin

1 tsp dried thyme

1 cinnamon stick

4 whole cloves
   or 4 pinches ground cloves

4 whole allspice berries
   or 4 pinches ground allspice

1 medium tomato, cut crosswise
   into ½-inch slices

3 medium tomatillos, cut
   crosswise into ½-inch slices

1 cup very hot vegetable broth or
   Simplicity Broth (page 57)

2 oz raw cacao paste sweetened
   with coconut sugar, chopped

1 Tbsp raw honey

1 tsp sea salt

• Chop the chilies and discard the stems and seeds. Place the remaining bits of chili in a dry medium skillet over low heat and toast for 2-3 minutes. Remove from heat.

• Transfer the toasted chilies to a high-power blender and add the cranberries. Set aside.

• Place a second skillet over low heat and warm the coconut oil. Add the onion and garlic and sauté for about 5 minutes. Add the cinnamon stick, macadamia nuts, sesame and pumpkin seeds, chipotle powder, cumin seeds, thyme, cloves, and allspice and sauté, stirring frequently, for 5 minutes, or until the onions are translucent and the mixture is very aromatic. Remove from heat. Discard the cinnamon stick and add the contents of the second skillet to the mixture in the blender.

• Return the dry skillet to medium heat. Add the tomato and tomatillo slices and blacken them for about 4-5 minutes on each side. Remove from heat and add contents to the mixture in the blender.

• Add hot vegetable broth, cacao paste, honey, and salt to the blender mixture and puree, first on low then gradually raising the speed to high, until well mixed.

• At this point, the sauce should be warm enough to serve. If making ahead of time, store in a glass container with a tight seal and gently reheat on the stove when needed.

UNFILTERED RAW HONEY IS TRULY A LONGEVITY-BOOSTING SUPERFOOD WHEN IT INCLUDES THE CAPPINGS, WHICH CONTAIN BITS OF POLLEN, BEESWAX, AND PROPOLIS. RAW HONEY HAS MANY MEDICINAL PROPERTIES, SUCH AS TREATING SORE THROATS AND COLDS, HEALING WOUNDS AND BURNS, AND CAN BE USED AS A FACIAL MASK, OR AS A PREMIUM SOURCE OF CALORIES FOR ATHLETES (THE ANCIENT GREEKS RESERVED HONEY FOR OLYMPIC COMPETITORS). AFTER HONEY IS COOKED, FILTERED, AND DILUTED, IT DOES NOT HAVE THE SAME NUTRITIONAL BENEFITS, AS HEAT DESTROYS THE ENZYMES, PROBIOTICS, AND VITAL NUTRIENTS.

CARROT ZIP-ZAP DRESSING

Makes 1½ cups

1 tsp coconut oil

2 medium shallots, chopped

2 medium carrots, peeled and chopped

3-inch piece fresh ginger, peeled and chopped

2 Tbsp unpasteurized white miso

2 Tbsp olive oil

2 Tbsp flaxseed oil

2 Tbsp lemon juice

2 tsp apple cider vinegar

¼ tsp salt

• In a small pan over medium heat, warm the coconut oil. Add the shallots and sauté for 3-5 minutes, or until lightly golden brown and fragrant.

• In a high-power blender, combine contents of the pan and the remaining ingredients and puree, first on low then gradually raising the speed to high, until smooth and creamy.

• Use immediately or transfer to a glass jar with a tight seal and store in the refrigerator for up to 5 days.

MELLOW WASABI DRESSING

Makes about 2½ cups

⅔ cup water

½ cup + 1 Tbsp flaxseed oil

½ cup fresh ginger, peeled and cubed

⅓ cup flat-leaf parsley, chopped

⅓ cup coconut oil

¼ cup lemon juice

1 Tbsp Bragg Liquid Aminos

2 Tbsp apple cider vinegar

2 Tbsp unpasteurized white miso

2 Tbsp raw honey

1 Tbsp sesame oil

1 tsp wasabi powder

1 clove garlic

¼ tsp freshly ground black pepper

• In a high-power blender, combine all ingredients and puree, first on low then gradually raising the speed to high, until smooth.

• Use immediately or transfer to a glass jar with a tight seal, and store in the refrigerator for up to 2 weeks.

BLACK SESAME BASIL MINT MOON CHEEZE

Can be served with crudités, dehydrated vegetable or seed crackers, and sliced heirloom tomatoes for an excellent appetizer or afternoon snack. Makes a yummy filling for sandwiches or nori rolls as well.

Makes about 1 cup

½ cup raw sunflower seeds, soaked 4-6 hours, drained, and rinsed

½ cup blanched almonds, soaked 4-6 hours, drained, and rinsed

1 Tbsp unpasteurized white miso

2 cups water

3 Tbsp lemon juice

¼ cup + 2 Tbsp olive oil

1 oz basil leaves

⅓ oz mint leaves, chiffonaded

1 clove garlic

1 clove black garlic

1 tsp Bragg Liquid Aminos

½ tsp salt

½ tsp nutritional yeast

2½ capsules Blue Majik

1-2 Tbsp black sesame seeds

• In a high-power blender, combine the sunflower seeds, almonds, miso, and water and blend to a fine slurry, but not a cream.

• Transfer mixture to a 1-quart jar with a lid and cover it with a screen or some cheesecloth. Set the jar in a warm place (e.g., on top of the refrigerator) and let it ferment for 8-12 hours, until the pulp has separated from the fluid and little bubbles have formed. Technically, it can go longer—up to 24 hours—but this will produce a stronger-smelling mixture. (If the mixture has fermented long enough and you don't have time to squeeze it, you can seal the lid and refrigerate it for up to a day, to slow the fermentation process.)

• Strain the mixture, 1 cup at a time, through a nut mylk bag, squeezing out and discarding the liquid. If it feels a little tingly, that means the probiotics are alive.

• Transfer the dry, crumbly bits to a food processor. Add lemon juice, 2 Tbsp oil, the basil, mint, garlic, Bragg Liquid Aminos, salt, yeast, and 2 capsules of the Blue Majik and process until the mixture becomes a fine, spreadable, blue-green cheeze.

• Press the mixture into a round mold or bowl and then flip it onto a plate, forming a dome. Top the cheeze dome with the remaining ¼ cup oil, ½ capsule Blue Majik, and sesame seeds.

• Serve immediately or transfer to a glass jar with a tight seal and store in the refrigerator for up to 4 days.

SHATAVARI GINGER HONEY BUTTER

A quixotic herbal concoction, this shape-shifting condiment can be enjoyed many ways—as a sweet center for chocolate truffles, slathered on toast, in a latte as a booster, or simply spooned straight from the jar.

Makes about 3 cups

⅔ cup nut mylk (pages 174, 177)

2-inch piece fresh ginger, peeled and sliced

1 Tbsp raw honey

4 oz coconut butter

3 oz raw cacao butter

3 Tbsp coconut oil

1 Tbsp tocotrienol flakes (vitamin E supplement)

1-2 tsp shatavari

¼ tsp ground vanilla beans

½ tsp salt

• In a high-power blender, combine nut mylk, ginger, and honey and puree until smooth. Gently strain mixture through a nut mylk bag to remove the ginger fibers.

• Over medium heat in a bain marie, a double boiler, or in a glass or metal mixing bowl placed atop a pot containing about 1 inch of hot water, melt together the coconut butter, cacao butter, coconut oil, tocotrienols, shatavari, vanilla, and salt.

• In a separate pot over low heat, warm the ginger–nut mylk to about the same temperature as the melted coconut-cacao mixture. Add the warmed nut mylk to the melted coconut-cacao mixture and gently stir for about 20-30 seconds, or until just mixed (do not overstir, or the mixture will seize up).

• Transfer to a sealed glass jar or butter molds and store in the refrigerator. Remove from the refrigerator 20 minutes prior to serving to soften. Can be stored for up to 5 days.

ALSO KNOWN AS WILD ASPARAGUS, SHATAVARI ROOT IS AN AYURVEDIC TONIC USED TO PRODUCE HORMONAL BALANCE, PARTICULARLY IN WOMEN, AND CAN PROVIDE MENOPAUSAL SUPPORT. IT HAS GROUNDING, COOLING EFFECTS ON THE BODY, AND SOOTHES DIGESTION WHILE SUPPORTING PERISTALSIS IN THE INTESTINES. SHATAVARI CAN MOISTURIZE A DRY RESPIRATORY TRACT, AND BRINGS IMMUNE-BOOSTING PROPERTIES AS WELL.

COUSINS TO TOCOPHEROLS, TOCOTRIENOLS ARE SYNERGISTIC COMPOUNDS FOUND IN VITAMIN E. TOCOTRIENOLS CAN PROVIDE THERAPEUTIC AND PREVENTIVE PROPERTIES AGAINST CANCER AS WELL AS CARDIOVASCULAR AND OTHER AGE-RELATED DISEASES THAT COMMON TOCOPHEROLS ALONE CANNOT PROVIDE. MOREOVER, TOCOTRIENOLS HAVE NEUROPROTECTIVE BENEFITS, AND CAN HELP THE BODY REBUILD ARTERIES AFTER A STROKE.

METRIC CONVERSIONS

VOLUME

1 tsp = ⅓ Tbsp = ⅙ fl oz = 4 ml

1 Tbsp = 3 tsp = ½ fl oz = 15 ml

⅛ cup = 2 Tbsp = 1 fl oz = 30 ml

¼ cup = 4 Tbsp = 2 fl oz = 50 ml

⅓ cup = ¼ cup + 4 tsp = 2¾ fl oz = 75 ml

½ cup = 8 Tbsp = 4 fl oz = 125 ml

¾ cup = 10 Tbsp = 6 fl oz = 175 ml

1 cup = ½ pint = 8 fl oz = 250 ml

1 pint = 16 fl oz = 2 cups = 500 ml

1 quart = 32 fl oz = 2 pints

1 liter = 34 fl oz = 1 quart + ¼ cup

1 gallon = 128 fl oz = 4 quarts

TEMPERATURE

450°F = 230°C

425°F = 220°C

400°F = 200°C

350°F = 180°C

325°F = 165°C

300°F = 150°C

250°F = 125°C

225°F = 110°C

MASS

½ oz = 14 grams

2 oz = 57 grams

3 oz = 85 grams

4 oz = 113 grams

5 oz = 142 grams

6 oz = 170 grams

8 oz = 227 grams

10 oz = 283 grams

12 oz = 340 grams

16 oz = 454 grams

INDEX

ABOUT THE AUTHORS

Catharina Hedberg grew up in Sweden, where from an early age she enjoyed all outdoor activities and especially hiking in the forest, where seasonally she could collect berries, mushrooms, and other eatables that nature provided. These experiences awakened a deep appreciation for all natural ways of creating health in body, mind, and soul. After graduating with a Master's degree in Physical Education and Physical Therapy, her adventurous spirit led Hedberg to create health programs around the world. In California, she met up with Anne Marie Bennstrom, a well-known Swedish pioneer in the health field. Sharing the same vision, they decided to open a small retreat to introduce a new natural concept of achieving great health on all levels, one guest at a time.

Since 2005 when she first met the founders, Suzie Spring Bohannon has felt drawn to the loving energy of The Ashram. They shared views on the transformative powers of hiking, laughter, and raw foods—and the joy that comes from sharing these gifts with others. Bohannon has developed a seasonal farm-to-table menu harvested from The Ashram's organic garden, combining bold flavors, superfoods, and nutritional philosophies from around the world, providing guests with a culinary adventure. With a playful approach to nutrition, she recognizes that food nourishes both body and soul as well as our connection to others, and she is delighted to share The Ashram's recipes in this book.

For eighteen years, Amy Neunsinger's photography has defined some of America's most influential style-based brands, including Avon, Clinique, Crate & Barrel, *House Beautiful*, *Martha Stewart Living*, Nordstrom, and West Elm. Her home and personal style have been featured on TV and in magazines including *Better Homes & Gardens*, *Blueprint*, and *Los Angeles Times*, and her work has appeared in popular books such as *Everyday Chic* (HarperCollins), *The Sprinkles Baking Book* (Grand Central), *Kitchen Revelry* (St. Martin's Press), *Shabby Chic Interiors* (CICO Books), *Nancy Silverton's Sandwich Book* (Knopf), and *Weeknights with Giada* (Clarkson Potter). She lives in Los Angeles with her husband and two sons.

Frances Boswell has worked with food since her first job at 15 as a chopper at a local restaurant, for which she wore swim goggles to protect her eyes from onion fumes. She became a chef for an adventure travel outfitter, then joined *Martha Stewart Living* as part of the start-up team. After serving as recipe developer and food stylist for publications including *Food & Wine, Gourmet,* and *Health,* Boswell became Food Director for *Real Simple.* Exploring food as it relates to health, she then studied acupuncture and Traditional Chinese Medicine. Boswell believes that for food to nourish both body and spirit, it must taste and look beautiful.

When Price Arana first arrived at The Ashram twenty years ago, she sensed a real power in the mountains, and the "spiritual boot camp" became her yearly retreat. Believing there is no place in the world quite like it, Arana approached Hedberg with the idea to create a cookbook, as a way to bring a little piece of The Ashram into people's homes. Arana owns The Press Cabinet, an advertising and marketing agency known for branding in highly creative and non-traditional ways. She has helmed several non-profit campaigns for various organizations and worthy causes, including bringing attention to the plight of victims of sex-trafficking, the Christopher & Dana Reeve Foundation, and Blessings in a Backpack. Arana recently co-directed and executive produced the documentary film *An Undeniable Voice.* She lives in Los Angeles with her two sons.

ABOUT THE ASHRAM

The Ashram opened its doors 1974 with the mission to introduce healthy habits to guests and educate them to make better choices. The first "Boot-Camp Health Retreat" with a simple formula of hiking, yoga, organic vegetarian food, and a genuine sense of heartfelt care. Physical movement in all forms and fresh beautifully served food is essential, but to us the most important ingredients are love and laughter. If the whole house is full of joy, we have in a small way succeeded in making a difference in someone's life.

ACKNOWLEDGMENTS

I want to express my gratitude to Anne Marie for holding the Light Energy and also to Pia and Matt Schwaiger for their love and support. Sincere thanks goes to everyone in my amazing staff who with their willingness, genuine care, and heartfelt love make The Ashram program a unique and soulful experience for every person who visits us. I appreciate all our guests who continue to come and let us participate in their life's journey. We love you and consider each one of you, returnee or new, to be part of our Ashram family. With love and gratitude, Catharina

We are so grateful to the amazing Assouline team and specifically to Prosper Assouline, Esther Kremer, Amy Slingerland, and Charlotte Sivriere. Endless thanks to The Press Cabinet team and especially to Angie Dingman, Cori Zuckerman Vallone, and Janet Kim. Much love and gratitude to Joaquin and Dashiell Arana. To Amy Neunsinger and Frances Boswell, thank you for bringing our food to life in these beautiful photos! XO, Price and Catharina

CREDITS

All photographs by Amy Neunsinger, except the following:
Endpapers, pages 14 middle row right bottom and bottom row left, 20-21, 98-99: Price Arana; pages 4-5: © Bob Rover/Alamy Stock Photo; pages 8, 10, 13, 14 top row left, 14 middle row left, 14 middle row right top, 18, 190 top: Matt Schwaiger; pages 14 top row middle, 17, 80-81, 164-165: Thomas Engstrom; page 14 center: courtesy of The Ashram; pages 14 bottom row right, 58-59, 124-125: Javiera Estrada; pages 40-41: Natasha Wilson; pages 146-147: © Zachary Frank/Alamy Stock Photo; page 190 middle: Into Life Photography; page 190 bottom: Toki Cavener; page 191 top: Ngoc Minh; page 191 bottom: Douglas Kirkland.

Special thanks to Perrin Davis, Starr Hackwelder at Alamy, and Stephanie Hardy for their assistance.